ON MARRIAGE
AND FAMILY

ON MARRIAGE AND FAMILY

Classic and Contemporary Texts

Edited by
Matthew Levering

A SHEED & WARD BOOK

ROWMAN & LITTLEFIELD PUBLISHERS, INC.

Lanham • Boulder • New York • Toronto • Oxford

A SHEED & WARD BOOK

ROWMAN & LITTLEFIELD PUBLISHERS, INC.

Published in the United States of America
by Rowman & Littlefield Publishers, Inc.
A wholly owned subsidiary of The Rowman & Littlefield Publishing Group, Inc.
4501 Forbes Boulevard, Suite 200, Lanham, Maryland 20706
www.rowmanlittlefield.com

PO Box 317
Oxford
OX2 9RU, UK

British Library Cataloguing in Publication Information Available

Library of Congress Cataloging-in-Publication Data

Levering, Matthew Webb, 1971-
 On marriage and family : classic and contemporary texts / Matthew Levering.
 p. cm.
 Includes bibliographical references and index.
 ISBN 0-7425-4248-3 (cloth : alk. paper) — ISBN 0-7425-4249-1
(pbk. : alk. paper)
 1. Marriage—Religious aspects—Christianity. 2. Family—Religious
aspects—Christianity. I. Title.
BV835.L475 2005
261.8'358—dc22   2004023041

∞™ The paper used in this publication meets the minimum requirements of
American National Standard for Information Sciences—Permanence of Paper
for Printed Library Materials, ANSI/NISO Z39.48-1992.

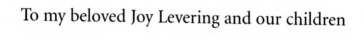

To my beloved Joy Levering and our children

Contents

Introduction

THE PRESENT BOOK TELLS THE STORY of the Christian understanding of marriage and the family, as presented by the great saints and teachers of the Church. Yet, is this a story worth learning about? After reading some literature on marriage, one might wonder. For instance, the early-twentieth-century curmudgeon and journalist H. L. Mencken, no friend of Christianity, once remarked, "Certainly the world should have learned by this time that theologians make a mess of everything they touch, including even religion. Yet in the United States they are still allowed, against all reason and experience, to have their say in a great variety of important matters, and everywhere they go they leave their sempiternal trail of folly and confusion. Why those of the Christian species should be consulted about marriage and divorce is more than I can make out."[1] More recently, Margaret Atwood's best-selling novel, *The Handmaid's Tale* (now also a critically acclaimed play), presents marriage—allegedly "Christian" marriage—in the darkest possible terms.

Because of its thoroughgoing criticisms, *The Handmaid's Tale* may serve as a starting point for exploring how Christian marriage has been conceived over 2,000 years and why that conception could cause offense to modern sensibilities—and yet also why the Christian understanding of marriage and the family remains *radically beautiful*.

---

[1] H. L. Mencken, *A Second Mencken Chrestomathy*, ed. Terry Teachout (New York: Vintage Books, 1994), 147.

In Atwood's cautionary tale of the future, biblical fundamentalists have taken over power and have remolded the institution of marriage, among other things, into a more "biblical" form. As in Abraham's day, there are now wives (e.g., Sarah), who have the social status, and handmaids (e.g., Hagar), whom the husbands, once a month and no more, seek to impregnate. The handmaids are discarded by being sent to the environmentally toxic "Colonies" once they reach menopause.

Offred, the protagonist of the story, is "among the first wave of women recruited for reproductive purposes and allotted to those who both required such services and could lay claim to them through their position in the elite."[2] These women are "recruited" by coercion: at first, they are women who either are in a second marriage, through divorce (now condemned) or widowhood, or are in a nonmarital heterosexual or homosexual liason (now condemned); and eventually they also include women whose marriages were contracted outside the state church. Such women become "handmaids" or slave-breeders for the elite men of the more "biblical" society. Breeders have been made necessary because of the sharp decline in Western birthrates.

The Christian fundamentalists seek to justify this employment of female breeders on biblical grounds. They condemn and outlaw artificial insemination and fertility clinics, along with (of course) birth control and abortion. A biblical loophole, however, is found for surrogate mothers, because of the precedent of Sarah's handmaid Hagar (Gen 16:2). We learn that the rulers—who call themselves "Commanders"—of what is now the "Republic of Gilead" "replaced the serial polygamy [divorce and remarriage] common in the pre-Gilead period with the older form of simultaneous polygamy practiced both in early Old Testament times and in the former state of Utah in the nineteenth century."[3] Closet progressives or liberals who step out of line, for instance by allowing handmaids to escape via the "Underground Femaleroad," are systematically purged in this new order.[4]

Near the story's end, Offred, thinking that she has avoided punishment for having an illicit sexual relationship with an elite man named Nick, reverts to the destructive self-abnegation that she has been taught:

---

[2] Margaret Atwood, *The Handmaid's Tale* (New York: Anchor Books, 1998), 304.

[3] Ibid., 305.

[4] Ibid., 309.

"Dear God, I think, I will do anything you like. Now that you've let me off, I'll obliterate myself, if that's what you really want; I'll empty myself, truly, become a chalice. I'll give up Nick, I'll forget about the others, I'll stop complaining. I'll accept my lot. I'll repent. I'll abdicate. I'll renounce."[5] The "God" whom she calls upon demands absolute "renouncing" of her will, which means, in the story, becoming a doormat to be abused by men. This "God," as understood in Gilead, requires the handmaids to be "two-legged wombs, that's all: sacred vessels, ambulatory chalices."[6] The language of sexual abuse is interwoven with the language of Christianity in the worldview into which the handmaids have been brainwashed.

It will be clear Atwood's cautionary tale is far closer to the Taliban than to Christian marriage. Abraham and Sarah's behavior toward Hagar is not approved in the Bible, where it is presented as a failure to trust that the Lord will provide a child as he has promised. Neither does Atwood's distortion of the Christian understanding of the self-gift fit with evangelical or Catholic understandings.

Yet, *The Handmaid's Tale* is effective in confronting us with some of the ways that Christian marriage is, indeed, quite radical as understood and practiced (however imperfectly!) in the 2,000-year Catholic tradition. As Atwood indicates, Christians have promoted the idea that marriage, once freely contracted, is *indissoluble*. Only thereby can the vulnerability of each partner, and of the children, be protected against the whims of sexual urges, midlife crises, and the like. Persons in marriage cannot be tossed aside like trash when no longer pleasing. When the Pharisees ask him whether divorce is lawful, Jesus Christ acknowledges that divorce was permissible in the Mosaic law, but he makes clear that divorce can no longer be permitted: "For your hardness of heart he [Moses] wrote you this commandment. But from the beginning of creation, 'God made them male and female.' 'For this reason a man shall leave his father and mother and be joined to his wife, and the two shall become one.' So they are no longer two but one. What therefore God has joined together, let not man put asunder" (Mk 10:5–9).

---

[5] Ibid., 286.
[6] Ibid., 136.

Aware of the difficulties involved with indissoluble marriage, Jesus' disciples later put the question to him again. Once more he offers a striking insistence upon the permanence of the gift of self of the two persons who freely accept each other, as later marriage rites put it, "for better or worse, for richer or poorer, in sickness and in health." The permanent gift of self is the mark of love, which cannot be manifested when one abandons the living person to whom one has freely committed oneself. Jesus tells his disciples, "Whoever divorces his wife and marries another, commits adultery against her; and if she divorces her husband and marries another, she commits adultery" (Mk 10:11–12). Human beings cannot be discarded so that one can move on to another mate. Love requires more; love requires even sacrifice in order to bear its true fruit.

G. K. Chesterton puts it this way: "The principle is this: that in everything worth having, even in every pleasure, there is a point of pain or tedium that must be survived, so that the pleasure may revive and endure. . . . In everything on this earth that is worth doing, there is a stage when no one would do it, except for necessity or honor. It is then that the Institution [of indissoluble marriage] upholds a man and helps him on to the firmer ground ahead."[7] While separation is permissible, remarriage after divorce is not.

Atwood also shows that Christian marriage is set apart by the importance it attaches to *children*. Jesus confirms the significance of children in a variety of ways. He instructs us to learn our spiritual attitude toward God from the confidence that young children have in their parents: "At that time the disciples came to Jesus, saying, 'Who is the greatest in the kingdom of heaven?' And calling to him a child, he put him in the midst of them, and said, 'Truly, I say to you, unless you turn and become like children, you will never enter the kingdom of heaven. Whoever humbles himself like this child, he is the greatest in the kingdom of heaven'" (Mt 18:1–4). In welcoming children into our midst, we thereby welcome Jesus himself: "Whoever receives one such child in my name receives me" (Mt 18:5).

Once, returning from a trip to a Latin American country, a friend told me that he had been amazed to see so many children there. Americans in non-Western countries are often shocked by the completely different view

---

[7] G. K. Chesterton, *What's Wrong with the World* (San Francisco: Ignatius Press, 1994 [1910]), 45.

of children that prevails in such countries. Thus an African man recently told me regarding the importance of children, "Who is going to smile at you at breakfast? Your bank account?" In contrast to societies with few children, a Christian culture should be one that, within marriage, generously welcomes children. In the contemporary world, where population growth seems a potential threat (among many others) to the Western economic standard of living, how much is being sacrificed in order for us to be materially wealthy? Jesus warns his disciples: "How hard it will be for those who have riches to enter the kingdom of God!" (Mk 10:23).

Jesus' love for children contrasts with contemporary views on limiting children for the sake of other lesser goods. The world was made for children. A task of Christian marriage has always been to recover, and exhibit, the beauty of children, in whom the self-giving love of the parents bears the unique fruit of new children of God. Indeed, the married couple themselves must learn from children how to live. Karol Wojtyla (now Pope John Paul II), in his play *The Jeweler's Shop*, has a man remark to his wife after years of troubled marriage: "What a pity that for so many years we have not felt ourselves to be a couple of children. Anna, Anna, how much we have lost because of that!"[8]

Similarly, the Christian view of self-giving love in marriage as, in the normal course of things, bearing fruit in children, also conflicts with Atwood's depiction of *abortion* as one form of birth control among others.

As a young man, I too accepted abortion. One day in college, however, as I was working on an essay on the abortion debate in the early 1970s for a history class, the thought struck me: "This means that my mother had the right to kill me in her womb." Suddenly, I was profoundly shocked and shaken to the core by the thought that my mother, or anyone else, had a supposed right to kill me as a fetus and dispose of me as trash.

It is also true that the seriousness with which sexual intercourse is approached in Christian marriage—namely as an act of radical self-giving love in which one loses oneself and fully gives oneself to the other—is profoundly at variance with Atwood's governing assumption that human sexuality ultimately boils down to pleasure, whether one's own or another's. Sexual intercourse in Christian marriage has to be conformed to self-giving love rather than to the selfishness that so easily

---

[8] Karol Wojtyla, *The Jeweler's Shop*, trans. Boleslaw Taborski (San Francisco: Ignatius Press, 1992), 91.

governs our lives. Couples who throw away their birth control in order to attempt to conceive a child know experientially the thrill of self-giving openness. Yet, the couple is free to abstain on rational grounds from sexual intercourse during periods of fertility ("Natural Family Planning"). This might sound difficult to those for whom sexual abstinence is difficult. And admittedly, Christian marriage is not supposed to be easy. As Jesus teaches, "If any man would come after me, let him deny himself and take up his cross and follow me" (Mt 16:24). The gift of self has to be total, and this gift will be at times sacrificial.

Jesus himself models sacrificial love for us and commands us to follow his example: "This is my commandment, that you love one another as I have loved you. Greater love has no man than this, that a man lay down his life for his friends" (Jn 15:12–13). Only by the grace of the Holy Spirit will we be able to live out marriages that are indissoluble, welcoming of children, and characterized intimately by the thrill of radically self-giving, open love. Yet, when we experience the gifts that Christian marriage brings, we will discover that these gifts are far more joyous and liberating than those that the world can offer—money, status, more things, etc. As St. Paul says, "So faith, hope, love abide, these three; but the greatest of these is love" (1 Cor 13:13).

Although Christian marriage involves self-sacrifice out of love, Atwood's presentation of Jesus' commandment of love *distorts* it by characterizing it as self-humiliation. Recall Offred's words to "God": "I'll obliterate myself. . . . I'll stop complaining. I'll accept my lot. I'll repent. I'll abdicate. I'll renounce."[9] Christian self-sacrifice does *not* mean denying that one has a self or rejecting oneself as worthless. On the contrary, what is involved here is the contrast between *selfish love* and *self-sacrificing love*. Anyone who has ever experienced love can testify that selfish love causes harm in the world, and self-sacrificing love (which requires mature self-possession) produces good effects both in the lover and in the world.

Those who follow Jesus by acting out of self-giving love find that, as Jesus promises, "whoever would save his life will lose it, and whoever loses his life for my sake will find it" (Mt 16:25). This is so because carrying one's cross is a sign of mature spiritual development, not of immature desire to become a doormat. Moreover, *both* partners in Chris-

---

[9] Atwood, 286.

tian marriage, not just the woman as Atwood's story suggests, must act with self-giving love toward the other and toward the children. Ultimately the couple will learn that such love, far from burdening them down, actually frees them. As Jesus says, "Take my yoke upon you, and learn from me; for I am gentle and lowly in heart, and you will find rest for your souls. For my yoke is easy, and my burden is light" (Mt 11:29–30).

In the Republic of Gilead, the elite males are "Commanders," while the elite women are defined by their relationship to men: "wives." This aspect is Atwood's treatment of the notion of male "headship" in Christian marriage. St. Paul teaches the doctrine of "headship" in Ephesians 5:

> Be subject to one another out of reverence for Christ. Wives, be subject to your husbands, as to the Lord. For the husband is the head of the wife as Christ is the head of the church, his body, and is himself its Savior. As the church is subject to Christ, so let wives also be subject in everything to their husbands. Husbands, love your wives, as Christ loved the church and gave himself up for her, that he might sanctify her, having cleansed her by the washing of water with the word, that he might present the church to himself in splendor, without spot or wrinkle or any such thing, that she might be holy and without blemish. Even so husbands should love their wives as their own bodies. He who loves his wife loves himself. For no man ever hates his own flesh, but nourishes and cherishes it, as Christ does the church, because we are members of his body. "For this reason a man shall leave his father and mother and be joined to his wife, and the two shall become one." This is a great mystery, and I mean in reference to Christ and the church; however, let each one of you love his wife as himself, and let the wife see that she respects her husband. (Eph 5:21–33)

What women require in Christian marriage, according to this passage, is to be truly loved, not used and discarded. It is well-known that men often use women sexually rather than treating women with love, and it is equally true that men often depend upon women to care for them (and the children and aging parents) without caring for women in return. Equally, what men need in marriage is to be respected and to be deemed worthy of trust and responsibility, the signs of true manhood.

St. Paul's main point, however, can easily be overlooked by focusing on the complementary ways that men and women in Christian marriage should treat each other. His main point is that men and women must "be subject to one another out of reverence for Christ" (Eph 5:21). By being "subject to one another" in self-sacrificing love, married couples share a love that is an image of the self-giving love that bonds Christ and his followers, the Church. As St. Paul encourages us, "Let all bitterness and wrath and anger and clamor and slander be put away from you, with all malice, and be kind to one another, tenderhearted, forgiving one another, as God in Christ forgave you" (Eph 4:31–32). These are the marks of Christian life and marriage, even though in practice, as weak sinners, Christians sometimes fall sadly short.

Throughout the 2,000 years of Christian history, Christians have reflected upon the meaning of marriage and the family. The fifteen selections in this volume, arranged chronologically, serve to guide the reader into the profundity of the Christian understanding of marriage as a permanent covenant of self-giving, fruitful love between a man and a woman. From the earliest Church, I have included excerpts from the writings of Hermas, St. Clement of Alexandria, and Tertullian. Hermas's *The Shepherd*, a popular spiritual handbook from the middle of the second century, witnesses to the Christian understanding of the indissolubility of marriage, and permits marrying again after the death of one's spouse. Writing in the late second century, St. Clement of Alexandria powerfully defends the goodness of marriage against the Gnostic thinkers who condemned marriage as sinful. Tertullian, who wrote a number of influential theological works in the early third century, compares the plight of pagan women, enslaved to the lusts of their husbands, to the glorious equality of Christian husband and wife. The excerpt from Tertullian is taken from a letter of his to his wife, whom he urges not to marry again after his death out of fear that a new husband might involve her in pagan practices.

From the Patristic period, which marks the high point of theological writing in the early Church, we find the writings of the friends St. Gregory of Nazianzus and St. Gregory of Nyssa, both of whom were bishops and theological writers during the enormously fertile fourth century. St. Gregory of Nazianzus extols the virtues of his married sister Gorgonia, and in the process makes clear that he possesses a strong sense of the beauty of her Christian marriage and of her dignity as a Christian woman, equal to any Christian man and superior to most. St. Gregory of Nyssa, himself a married man, explains why Christians value the practice of consecrated virginity. As he points out, marriage hardly needs defenders, since the great majority marry. Much ink was spilled in the early Church in order to show that the life of consecrated virginity possesses certain spiritual advantages that show that neither women nor men can be understood as if their duty was simply to produce as many children as possible—which was how pagan culture had valued women. From the same century, another great bishop-theologian, St. Augustine, describes how lust—treating women as simply to be used sexually—led him astray as a young man, due in part to the bad example of his father. In profound contrast, he also describes how his mother, a holy woman, prayed and worked for her son's conversion, and thereby supremely modeled for Augustine the Christian life.

From the medieval period, I have selected three different genres of writing. First, Hugh of St. Victor (a twelfth-century theologian) discusses in a scholastic fashion how marriage is both a bodily and a spiritual sacrament of union. He rejects any idea of marriage that would limit it to mere instrumentality, or bodily servitude, of one party to another. Second, St. Thomas Aquinas, who died in 1274, comments in a work of biblical exegesis on Jesus' miracle at the wedding at Cana as depicted in the Gospel of John. Here again we find marriage as an image of the spiritual marriage between God and humankind. Lastly, from the hagiographical *Life* of the fourteenth-century foundress and reformer St. Birgitta of Sweden, who was married and had eight children, we learn the story of how she managed family life and guided her husband in the paths of holiness as he approached his death. All three writings demonstrate the profound integration, in the minds of Christians, between marriage and human holiness.

From the Reformation and Early Modern period, St. Thomas More instructs the tutor of his daughter on the equality of women and men, and of the fundamental importance of avoiding pride. Similarly, St. Teresa of Avila bemoans the fact that she did not follow the example of the humility of her parents, but instead fell into pride and frivolity. From the following century, the seventeenth, St. Jane de Chantal, who was married with a large family, offers practical and spiritual advice to one of her married daughters. In every case, what becomes clear is how deeply, for these Christian saints, family life—the life of marriage—must be infused by the Christian principles of self-giving love and humility, if the equality and dignity of men and women are to be truly respected and fostered.

Finally, the Modern period contains an excerpt from the Second Vatican Council along with excerpts from the writings of two of the most revered Christians of the late twentieth century, Pope John Paul II and Mother Teresa. The selection from *Gaudium et Spes*, Vatican II's pastoral constitution on the Church and the modern world, emphasizes the distinctiveness of Christian marriage, characterized by radical gift of self on the part of both spouses. Pope John Paul II, in a set of discourses taken from his weekly audiences on "The Theology of the Body" in the early 1980s, contrasts true love in marriage with the lust that distorts relationships between men and women into relationships of oppressive domination and use, rather than expressions of the communion of persons to which rational creatures are called.

As the last selection in the book, Mother Teresa's famous speech before the National Prayer Breakfast in Washington, D.C., encapsulates her understanding of the spiritual riches available through Christian marriages in which children are freely welcomed. In this way, she argues, poor countries, and impoverished peoples, are often spiritually wealthier than their materially rich counterparts. For these twentieth-century thinkers, the sign of distinctive Christian marriage is a self-giving communion of persons that exhibits and images the spiritual wealth and fruitfulness of the divine communion of Persons. The Christian tradition of reflection on marriage is united in seeing it as a place of spiritual growth between equals, in which mutual sacrifice is called for in order to attain the goods that God desires for his creatures.

Hermas

The identity of the author of *The Shepherd,* a popular devotional book of the mid-second century, is not known. The book was treated with esteem by St. Irenaeus and other early theologians. According to some sources, Hermas was the brother of Pope Pius I (died c. 154), and had been a slave who had earned his freedom, married, and raised a family. The book was best known for its moral teachings, which are in evidence in the excerpt below directing the Christian to practice chaste and indissoluble marriage.

"I CHARGE YOU," SAID HE [the Shepherd], "to guard your chastity, and let no thought enter your heart of another man's wife, or of fornication, or of similar iniquities; for by doing this you commit a great sin. But if you always remember your own wife, you will never sin. For if this thought enters your heart, then you will sin; and if, in like manner, you think other wicked thoughts, you commit sin. For this thought is great sin in a servant of God. But if any one commits this wicked deed, he works death for himself. Attend, therefore, and refrain from this thought; for where purity dwells, there iniquity ought not to enter the heart of a righteous man." I said to him, "Sir, permit me to ask you a few questions." "Say on," said he. And I said to him, "Sir, if any one has a wife who trusts in the Lord, and if he detects her in adultery, does the

From "The Shepherd of Hermas," trans. F. Crombie, in *Ante-Nicene Fathers,* ed. Alexander Roberts and James Donaldson, vol. 2, *Fathers of the Second Century: Hermas, Tatian, Athenagoras, Theophilus, and Clement of Alexandria* (Peabody, Mass.: Hendrickson, 1995 [1885]), 21–22.

man sin if he continues to live with her?" And he said to me, "As long as he remains ignorant of her sin, the husband commits no transgression in living with her. But if the husband knows that his wife has gone astray, and if the woman does not repent, but persists in her fornication, and yet the husband continues to live with her, he also is guilty of her crime, and a sharer in her adultery." And I said to him, "What then, sir, is the husband to do, if his wife continue in her vicious practices?" And he said, "The husband should put her away, and remain by himself. But if he puts his wife away and marries another, he also commits adultery." And I said to him, "What if the woman put away should repent, and wish to return to her husband: shall she not be taken back by her husband?" And he said to me, "Assuredly. If the husband does not take her back, he sins, and brings a great sin upon himself; for he ought to take back the sinner who has repented. But not frequently. For there is but one repentance to the servants of God. In case, therefore, that the divorced wife may repent, the husband ought not to marry another, when his wife has been put away. In this matter man and woman are to be treated exactly in the same way. Moreover, adultery is committed not only by those who pollute their flesh, but by those who imitate the heathen in their actions. Wherefore if any one persists in such deeds, and repents not, withdraw from him, and cease to live with him, otherwise you are a sharer in his sin. Therefore has the injunction been laid on you, that you should remain by yourselves, both man and woman, for in such persons repentance can take place. But I do not," said he, "give opportunity for the doing of these deeds, but that he who has sinned may sin no more. But with regard to his previous transgressions, there is One who is able to provide a cure; for it is He, indeed, who has power over all."

[. . .]

And again I asked him, saying, "Sir, since you have been so patient in listening to me, will you show me this also?" "Speak," said he. And I said, "If a wife or husband dies, and the widower or widow marries, does he or she commit sin?" "There is no sin in marrying again," said he; "but if they remain unmarried, they gain greater honor and glory with the Lord; but if they marry, they do not sin. Guard, therefore, your chastity and purity, and you will live to God. What commandments I now give you, and what I am to give, keep from henceforth, yea, from the very day when you were entrusted to me, and I will dwell in your house. And your former sins will be forgiven, if you keep my commandments. And all shall be forgiven who keep these my commandments, and walk in this chastity."

1. What does the Shepherd teach about repentance?
2. What is included within marital "chastity" according to the Shepherd?

St. Clement of Alexandria

St. Clement of Alexandria (c. 150–c. 220), a convert to Christianity probably born in Athens, taught in Alexandria until around 202 and died in Antioch. He stands out among the great theologians of the school of Alexandria (including such figures as Origen and St. Athanasius). Well versed in Greek philosophy, he presents Christ, the divine Word, as humankind's Teacher, and Christianity as the true "gnosis" or knowledge. The following excerpts from his writings defend marriage against "Gnostic" heretics, prominent in his day, who denied the goodness of marriage.

So NO ONE SHOULD EVER THINK that marriage under the rule of the Logos [Christ] is a sin, if he does not find it bitter to bring up children; indeed, for many people, childlessness is the most grievous experience of all. At the same time, if he does not regard the production of children as bitter because it drags him away from the things of God, for which there is necessarily no time, but does not look favorably upon life as a bachelor, then he can look forward to marriage, since there is no harm in disciplined pleasure, and each of us is in a position to make a decision over the engendering of children. I realize that there are some people who have used the excuse of marriage to abstain from it without following the principles of sacred knowledge and have fallen into hatred of humankind so that the spirit of Christian love has vanished from

From *Stromateis: Books One to Three*, trans. John Ferguson, vol. 85 of the Fathers of the Church Series (Washington, D.C.: The Catholic University of America Press, 1991), 297–299, 304–326. Used with permission: The Catholic University of America Press, Washington, D.C.

them; others have become embroiled in marriage and indulged their taste for pleasure within the authority of the Law, and as the prophet says, "have become like cattle" (Ps 49:12, 20).

Who are the two or three who gather in the name of Christ with the Lord in their midst (Mt 18:20)? By three does he not mean husband, wife, and child? A wife is united with her husband by God (Prov 19:14). But if a man wishes to be unencumbered, and prefers to avoid producing children because of the time it takes up, then, says the Apostle, "he had better stay unmarried like me" (1 Cor 7:8). Their interpretation of the Lord's meaning is this. In relation to the plurality, he is speaking of the creator, who is responsible for all coming into being; in relation to the one, he is speaking of the savior of the elect, naturally the son of a different god, of course, the good god. This is wrong. God through his Son is with those who responsibly marry and produce children, and it is the same God who in the same way is with the man who shows self-control in the light of the Logos. Another interpretation would make the three temper, desire, and reason; yet another flesh, soul, and spirit.

Perhaps the group of three of which we have been speaking is first an allusion to those called; secondly, to the elect; and thirdly, to the class of beings ordained to the highest honor. The power of God watching over all things is with them, indivisibly divided among them. So a person who makes proper use of the natural powers of the soul has a desire for appropriate objects but hates all that would injure, as the commandments prescribe. Scripture says, "You shall bless anyone who blesses you and curse anyone who curses you" (Gen 12:3, 27:29). But when a person has risen above temper and desire, when he shows an actual love for the creation, for the sake of God the maker of all things, then he will live a life of true knowledge, effortlessly embracing the state of self-control following the likeness of the Savior, bringing knowledge, faith, and love into a single unity. From that point he is single in judgment and genuinely spiritual. He is totally closed to thoughts which arise from temper or desire. He is being brought to perfection according to the image of the Lord by the actual craftsman, becoming a fully mature human being (Eph 4:13), at last worthy to be called brother by the Lord (Heb 2:11). He is at once friend and son to him. In this way the two or three are gathered into the same point, the truly Gnostic human being.

The concord of several, counting on the basis of the three with whom the Lord is found, may refer to the one Church, the one human being, the one race. Or perhaps the Lord in giving the Law was with the one people, the Jewish. When he was responsible for prophecy and sent Jeremiah to Babylon, and further called people from the gentiles through prophecy, he gathered together the two peoples (Eph 2:15). The third is surely the one who is formed out of the two into a new human being, in whom he walks and lives (2 Cor 6:16)—the very Church. The Law and the prophets are brought together with the gospel too, in the name of Christ into one true knowledge. So those who out of hatred refrain from marriage or misuse their physical being indiscriminately, out of desire, are not in the number of the saved with whom the Lord is found.

[…]

It is a lesson in self-discipline if physical union "is given a rest by agreement to allow time for prayer" (1 Cor 7:5). He appends the words "by agreement" to prevent a dissolution of the marriage and "time for" to prevent the husband who is forced to practice celibacy from slipping into sin, falling in love elsewhere while refraining from his own wife. By the same argument he said that the man who supposes that he is acting wrongly in bringing up his daughter as a virgin will properly give her away in marriage (1 Cor 7:36). One man may make himself celibate; another may join in marriage in order to have children. Both ought to have the end in view of remaining firmly opposed to any lower standard. If a person is going to be capable of keeping his life strict he is going to achieve greater worth for himself in God's eyes since his self-control combines chastity and rationality. If he goes beyond the rule to which he has committed himself with a view to greater renown, then he is liable to fall short in relation to his hopes. Celibacy and marriage have their distinctive services of the Lord, their different ministries. I am referring to the care of wife and children. The peculiar quality of the married state is the opportunity it gives for the man who seeks fulfillment through marriage to accept the overseeing of everything in the common home. The Apostle says bishops should be appointed from those who have learned by practice in their own home the charge of the whole Church (1 Tim 3:4–5). So each person should fulfill his service by the work in which he was called, so that he may be free in Christ and receive the appropriate reward for that service.

Yet again in speaking about the Law he makes use of an analogy. "The married woman," he says, "is tied to her husband by law during his lifetime" (Rom 7:2), and so on. And again, "The wife is under the marriage bond as long as her husband is alive. If he dies she is free to marry, provided it is in the Lord. But in my view her greatest blessing is to remain as she is" (1 Cor 7:39–40). Now, in the former passage he says, "You have died to the Law"—not to marriage!—"with a view to becoming another's, one who belongs to him was raised from the dead," at once Bride and Church. The Bride and Church must be pure alike from inward thoughts contrary to truth and from outward tempters, that is, the adherents of heretical sects who try to persuade her to sexual unfaithfulness to her one and only husband almighty God. We must not be led, "as the snake seduced Eve" (2 Cor 11:3), whose name means "Life" (Gen 3:20), to transgress the commandments under the influence of the wicked lewdness of the factions. The second passage established monogamy. We are not to suppose, in agreement with some people's exegesis, that the bond tying the wife to the husband means the involvement of the flesh with decay. He is assailing the view of those atheists who attribute the invention of marriage directly to the devil. This is a view which comes dangerously near to a slander against the lawgiver.

The Syrian Tatian, as I see it, had the effrontery to make this sort of thing his creed. Anyway, he writes in his work *On Training Following the Savior*, and I quote, "Agreement conduces to prayer. The common experience of corruption means an end to intercourse. At any rate, his acceptance of it is so grudging that he is really saying No to it altogether. He agreed to their coming together again because of Satan and because of weakness of will, but he showed that anyone who is inclined to succumb is going to be serving two masters (Mt 6:24), God when there is agreement, and weakness of will, sexual immorality, and the devil when there is not." He says this in his exegesis of the Apostle. He is playing intellectual tricks with the truth in seeking to establish a false conclusion on the basis of truth. We too agree that weakness of will and sexual immorality are passions inspired by the devil, but the harmony of responsible marriage occupies a middle position. When there is self-control it leads to prayer; when there is reverent bridal union, to childbearing. At any rate, there is a proper time for the breeding of children, and Scripture calls it knowledge, in the words, "Adam knew his wife Eve, and she conceived and bore a son, and called him by the name of Seth, 'for God has raised up for me another child in Abel's place'" (Gen 4:25). You see who is the target of the slanders of those who show their disgust at responsible marriage and attribute the process of birth to the devil? Scripture does not merely refer to "a god." By application of the definite article it indicates the almighty ruler of the universe.

The Apostle's added reference to their "coming together again because of Satan" is designed to anticipate and cut at the roots of any possibility of turning aside to other love affairs. The temporary agreement serves to negate natural desires but does not cut them out root and branch. These are why he reintroduces the marriage bond, not for uncontrolled behavior or sexual immorality or the operations of the devil, but to prevent him from falling under their sway. Tatian makes a distinction between the old humanity and the new, but it is not ours. We agree with him in that we too say that the old humanity is the Law, the new is the gospel. But we do not agree with his desire to abolish the Law as being the work of a different god. It is the same man, the same Lord who makes old things new. He no longer approves of polygamy (at that time God required it because of the need for increased numbers). He introduces monogamy for the production of children and the need to look after the home. Woman was offered as a "partner" in this (Gen 2:18). And if a man cannot control himself and is burning with passion so that the Apostle "out of sympathy" offers him a second marriage (1 Cor 7:9, 36), then he is not committing sin according to the Covenant, since it is not forbidden by the Law, but neither is he fulfilling the highest pitch of the gospel ethic. He is acquiring heavenly glory for himself, if he remains single and keeps immaculate the union which has been broken by death and cheerfully obeys what God has in store for him, becoming "undistracted" from the Lord's service (1 Cor 7:35). In the past, a man coming from marital intercourse was required to wash (Lev 15:18). It cannot be too strongly said that the Providence of God revealed through the Lord no longer makes this demand. The Lord eliminates washing after intercourse as unnecessary since he has cleansed believers by one single baptism for every such encounter, just as he takes in the many washings prescribed by Moses by one single baptism.

In the past, the Law prescribed washing after the generative deposit of seed in prophecy of our regeneration through the analogy of physical birth. It did not do so from distaste for the birth of a human being. The deposit of the seed makes possible the thing which emerges as a human being. It is not frequent acts of intercourse which promise birth; it is the acceptance of the seed by the womb. In nature's studio the seed is molded into an embryo. How can marriage in the past be a mere invention of the

Law, and marriage as ordained by our Lord be different, when it is the same God whom we worship? "Man must not pull apart that which God has joined together" (Mt 19:6). That is reasonable. Far more so that that Son will preserve the things which the Father has ordained. If the Law and gospel come from the same being, the Son cannot fight against himself. The Law is alive because it is spiritual (Rom 7:14), if we interpret it in the light of true knowledge. But we "have died to the Law through Christ's body with a view to belonging to another, the one who was raised from the dead," the one who was prophesied by the Law, "so that we may bear fruit for God" (Rom 7:4).

So "the Law is holy; the commandment is holy, righteous and good" (Rom 7:12). We died to the Law, that is to say, to the sin exposed by the Law, which the Law does not engender but reveals. It enjoins what we ought to do and bans what we ought not to do. It shows up the sin that is hidden, "so that sin may be seen for what it is" (Rom 7:14). But if legally constituted marriage is sin, I do not know how anyone can claim to know God while saying that God's commandment is sin. If the Law is holy, marriage is holy. Accordingly, the Apostle points this mystery in the direction of Christ and the Church (Eph 5:32). Just as "that which is born of the flesh is flesh, so that which is born of the Spirit is Spirit" (Jn 3:6), not just in the process of birth but in its education. So "the children are holy" (1 Cor 7:14), objects of delight, when the Lord's words have brought the soul to God as a bride. Anyway, there is a distinction between fornication and marriage, as great as separates the devil from God. "So you too have died to the Law through Christ's body with a view to belonging to another, the one who was raised from the dead" (Rom 7:4). It is implied that you have become attentive in your obedience, since it is actually congruent with the truth of the Law that we are servants of the same Lord who gives us his instructions at a distance.

No question but that it is reasonable for the Spirit to say explicitly of people like that "that in the last days people will abandon the faith and attach themselves to deceitful spirits and the teachings of demonic powers, under the influence of hypocritical liars who are corrupt in conscience and try to put an end to marriage. They teach abstinence from foods which God created to be gratefully enjoyed by believers who have acquired an inward knowledge of the truth. Everything created by God is good. None is to be rejected provided it is taken in a spirit of gratitude. It is sanctified by God's Word and by prayer" (1 Tim 4:1–5). It follows of necessity that there is no ban on marriage, or eating meat, or drinking wine, for it is written, "It is good to refrain from eating meat and drinking wine," if a person might give offense by eating, and, "It is good to stay as I am" (Rom 14:21; 1 Cor 7:8). But both the person who takes his food gratefully, and the one who equally gratefully abstains with an enjoyment marked by self-discipline must follow the Logos in their lives.

In general, all the Apostle's letters teach responsible self-control. They embrace thousands of instructions about marriage, the production of children, and domestic life. Nowhere do they blackball marriage, provided that it is responsible. They preserve the connection between the Law and the gospel. They welcome the man who embarks responsibly on marriage with gratitude to God, and the man who takes celibacy as his life companion in accordance with the Lord's will, each, as he has been called, making his choice in maturity and firmness. "Jacob's land was praised above any other land," says the prophet, glorifying the instrument of the Spirit. But there is a man who runs down birth, describing it as subject to decay and death, who forces things, and suggests that the Savior was speaking about having children in saying that we should not store treasure on earth, where it grows rusty and moth-eaten, and who is not ashamed to set alongside these the prophet's words: "You shall all grow old like clothes, and the moth will feed on you" (Is 50:9). We do not contradict Scripture. Our bodies are subject to decay and are naturally unstable. Perhaps he might be prophesying decay to his audience because they were sinners. The Savior was not speaking about having children. He was encouraging sharing of resources in those who wanted only to amass vast amounts of wealth rather than offer help to those in need.

That is why he says, "Do not work for perishable food, but for the food which lasts into eternal life" (Jn 6:27). Similarly, they cite the dictum "The children of this age do not marry and are not given in marriage" (Lk 20:35). But if anyone ponders over this answer about the resurrection of the dead, he will find that the Lord is not rejecting marriage, but is purging the expectation of physical desire in the resurrection. The words "The children of this age" were not spoken in contrast with the children of some other age. It is like saying, "Those born in this generation," who are children by force of birth, being born and engendering themselves, since without the process of birth no one will pass into this life. But this process of birth is balanced by a process of decay, and is no longer in store for the person who has once been cut off from life here. "You have one single Father in heaven"—and he is also, as creator, Father of all. "Do not call anyone on earth Father," he says (Mt 23:9). That is like saying that you are not to think of the man who sowed you by a physical process as responsible for your existence, but as a fellow worker, or rather a subordinate, in bringing you to birth.

In this way he wants us to turn back and become like children again (Mt 18:3), children who have come to know their real Father, come to a new birth by means of water, a method of birth quite different from that in the material creation. "Yes," he says, "the man who is unmarried cares for the Lord's business, the man who is married cares how to give his wife pleasure" (1 Cor 7:32–33). Well? Is it impossible to give pleasure to one's wife in ways acceptable to God and at the same time to show gratitude to God? Is it impermissible for the married man to have a partnership with his wife in looking after the Lord's business? But just as "the unmarried woman is looking after the Lord's business in seeking to be holy in body and spirit" (1 Cor 7:34), so the married woman cares in the Lord for her husband's business and the Lord's business in seeking to be holy in body and spirit. Both are holy in the Lord, one as a wife, the other as a virgin. But the Apostle fittingly pronounces humiliating opposition at full pitch to those who incline to second marriage. He is quick to say, "Every other sin is outside the body. Sexual promiscuity is a sin against one's own body" (1 Cor 6:18).

If anyone goes so far as to call marriage fornication, he is once more reverting to blasphemous slander upon the Law and the Lord. Avarice is called fornication because it is the opposite of self-sufficiency. Idolatry is called fornication because it is a spreading out from one God to many gods. In the same way, fornication takes place when a person falls away from a single marriage to a plurality. As we have remarked, the Apostle employs the words fornication and adultery in three senses. It is in relation to these matters that the prophet says, "It was through your own sins that you were sold," and again, "You experienced defilement in an alien land" (Is 50:1; Bar 3:10). He is applying the idea of defilement to a partnership involving an alien body rather than the body given away in marriage for the purpose of producing children. This is why the Apostle says, "So it is my wish that younger women should marry, have children, and be mistresses of their homes, without giving any opponent an opportunity to criticize. There are some already who have taken the wrong course and followed Satan" (1 Tim 5:14–15).

In fact, he expresses approval of the man who is husband of a single wife, whether elder, deacon, or layman, if he gives no ground for criticism in his conduct of his marriage (Tit 1:6; 1 Tim 3:2,12). He "will find salvation in bringing children into the world" (1 Tim 2:15). Once again the Savior calls the Jews "a wicked and adulterous generation" (Mt 12:39). He is teaching that they do not know the Law in the way the Law requires. By following the tradition of other generations and the commandments of human beings they were committing adultery against the Law, denying that it was given as lord and master of their virginity. Perhaps he also knew that they were slaves to strange desires, which led them into unswerving slavery to sins so that they were sold to foreigners. Among the Jews there were no publicly appointed prostitutes; adultery was in fact forbidden (Ex 20:14). The man who said, "I have married a wife and cannot come" (Lk 14:20) to the dinner offered by God was an example to expose those who were apostates to God's command for pleasures' sake; for on this argument neither those who were righteous before the coming of Christ nor those who have married after his coming will be saved, even if they are apostles. If they again adduce the well-known words of the prophet, "I have grown old amongst all my enemies" (Ps 6:8), by "enemies" they ought to understand "sins." There is one sin, and it is not marriage but fornication, or they would make a sin out of birth and birth's creator.

In such ways Julius Cassian, the founder of docetism, argues his case. Anyway, in his book *On Self-Control* or *On Celibacy* he says, and I quote, "No one should say that because we have the parts of the body that we do, with the female shaped one way and the male another, one for receiving, the other for inseminating, sexual intercourse has God's approval. For if this disposition was from the God towards whom we are eagerly pressing, he would not have blessed eunuchs (Mt 19:12), and the prophet would not have said that they are 'not an unfruitful tree' (Is 56:3), taking an analogy from the tree for the man who by deliberate choice emasculates himself from ideas of this sort."

In an effort to defend his godless opinion he adds, "How would it be unreasonable to bring a charge against the Savior if he malformed us and then freed us from his mistake and from partnership with our genitals, appendages and private parts?" In this view he is close to Tatian.

But he left Valentinus' school. That is why Cassian says, "When Salome asked when she would know the answer to her question the Lord replied, 'When you trample underfoot the integument of shame, and when the two become one and the male is one with the female, and there is no more male and female.'"

First then, we do not find this saying in our four traditional Gospels, but in the *Gospel according to the Egyptians*. Next, he does not seem to me to recognize that allusively the male impulse is temper, the female, desire. When these are at work, repentance and shame follow. So when a person refuses to indulge temper or desire, which in fact grow from bad character and bad nurture till they overshadow and conceal rational thought, when he strips off the darkness these produce, when he repents and out of repentance feels shame, when he integrates soul and spirit in obedience to the Word, then, as Paul joins in affirming, "there is no male or female among you" (Gal 3:28). The soul stands aside from the mere appearance of shape whereby male is distinguished from female, and is transformed into unity, being neither male nor female. But our brilliant friend must take a more Platonic view and imagine that the soul is divine in origin and has come to our world of birth and decay after being made effeminate by desire.

Then he does violence to Paul, in suggesting that he says that birth was constituted out of deceit. He is interpreting the words "My fear is that, just as the snake deceived Eve, your thoughts may be corrupted and diverted from a simple commitment to Christ" (2 Cor 11:3). Besides, the Lord by general agreement came for the wanderers, but they had not wandered from above to be born on earth (for birth, itself a creator, is a creation of the almighty, who would never drive the soul down from a better home to a worse). But the savior came for those who were wandering in thought, for us. Our thoughts were corrupted by our love of pleasure and our neglect of the commandments. Perhaps too the first-formed human anticipated the appropriate moment, coveted the grace of marriage before time, and so committed sin, since "everyone who looks at a woman with an eye to lust has already committed adultery with her" (Mt 5:28) in not waiting for the right moment of rational will.

It was the same Lord who at that time also gave judgment on the desire which anticipates marriage. So when the Apostle says, "Put on the new humanity created after God's way" (Eph 4:24), he is addressing us; we were shaped as we are by the Almighty's will. When he speaks of "old" and "new," he is not referring to birth and rebirth, but to disobedient and obedient ways of living. Cassian thinks the "tunics of skins" (Gen 3:21) are our bodies. We shall demonstrate later that he and those who argue like him are wrong in this, when we put our hands to the exposition of the genesis of humankind after the essential prolegomena. He goes on to say, "Those who are ruled by earthly values are born and engender. Our citizenship is in heaven and we welcome our Savior from there." We know this is well said, since we have a duty to behave as "temporarily resident aliens" (Heb 11:13); if we were married, as if we were single; if we have possessions, as if dispossessed; if we produce children, doing so in the knowledge that they will die; ready to give up our property, live without a wife if need be; dispassionate in our approach to the created world, with a mind above these things and a deep gratitude.

Again, when Paul says, "It is good for a man not to have contact with a woman, but to avoid immorality let each have his own wife," he offers a kind of exegesis by saying further, "to prevent Satan from tempting you." In the words "by using your lack of self-control" (1 Cor 7:5) he is addressing not those who practice marriage through self-control solely for the production of children, but those with a passionate desire to go beyond the production of children. He does not want the Adversary to create a hurricane so that the waves drive their yearnings to alien pleasure. It may be that Satan is jealous of those whose lives are morally upright, opposes them, and wants to master them. That is why he wishes to subject them to his command and aims to provide a jumping-off point by making self-control laborious.

So it is reasonable of Paul to say, "It is better to marry than to burn with passion" (1 Cor 7:9). He wants the husband to pay due attention to his wife and *vice versa*. He does not want them to deprive one another of the help offered towards childbirth through divine dispensation. They quote the words "Anyone who does not hate father or mother, wife or children, cannot be my disciple" (Lk 14:26). This is not an exhortation to hate your family, since Scripture says, "Honor your father and mother, for it to be well with you" (Ex 20:12). What he is saying is, "Do not be led astray by irrational impulses, and do not get involved in ordinary worldly practices." A family constitutes a household, and secular communities are made up of households. Paul says of those who find marriage a full-time occupation that they are "concerned to satisfy the world" (1 Cor 7:33). Again the Lord says, "Anyone married should not seek divorce; anyone unmarried should not seek marriage"—in other words, if a man has taken a public commitment to celibacy he should remain unmarried.

Anyway, the same Lord gives corresponding promises to both through the prophet Isaiah in saying, "The eunuch should not say, 'I am a barren tree.' This is what the Lord says to eunuchs: If you keep my sabbath and fulfill all my ordinances, I will give you a place which is preferable to sons and daughters" (Is 56:3–5). To be a eunuch does not of itself make a person righteous, still less the eunuch's keeping of the Sabbath, unless he performs the commandments. To the married he adds these words: "My elect shall not labor in vain or produce children to be under a curse, since their seed is blessed by the Lord" (Is 65:23). If a man produces children in obedience to the Logos, nurtures them, and educates them in the Lord, as with the man who fathers children following instruction in the truth, there is a reward in store for him, as for the elect seed too. Some people accept the view that the production of children is a curse; they do not understand that it is against these very people that Scripture is speaking. The Lord's true elect do not dogmatize or produce children to be under a curse; they leave that to the heretical sects.

So "eunuch" does not mean the man who has been physically emasculated, still less the unmarried man, but the man who is sterile in relation to truth. Previously he was "a barren tree." Once he has obeyed the Word and observed the sabbaths, put his sins to one side and fulfilled the commandments, he will be in greater honor than those whose education is theoretical and lack a proper way of living. "Little children," says the Teacher, "I am with you only a little longer" (Jn 13:33). That is why Paul says in his letter to Galatians, "My little children, I am going through the pains of childbirth with you a second time until Christ is formed in you" (Gal 4:19). Yet again in writing to the Corinthians he says, "You may have thousands of tutors in Christ but only one father. I am your father in Christ through the gospel" (1 Cor 4:15). This is why "no eunuch shall enter God's assembly" (Deut 23:1), being unproductive and unfruitful in behavior and speech. But "those who have made themselves eunuchs"—free from every sin—"for the kingdom of heaven's sake" (Mt 19:12), in fasting from worldliness, find blessing.

"Accursed be the day on which I was born—may it never be blessed," says Jeremiah (Jer 20:14). He is not simply saying that birth is an accursed thing; he has withdrawn in impatience at the sinful disobedience of the people. Anyway he goes on, "Why was I born to see trouble and toil? Why have my days come to fulfillment in shame?" (Jer 20:18) All those who preached the truth were in danger of persecution through the disobedience of their audience. "Why did my mother's womb not become my tomb, to prevent me from seeing Jacob's trials and the troubles of the house of Israel?" says the prophet Esdras. "No one is pure from stain," says Job, "not even if his life is only of one day's duration" (Job 14:4–5). It is for them to tell us how the newly born child could commit fornication or in what way the child who has never done anything at all has fallen under Adam's curse. The only thing left for them to say and still be consistent, I suppose, is that birth is evil not just for the body but for the soul for which the body exists. When David says, "I was brought into being in sin; my mother conceived me in disobedience to the Law" (Ps 51:5), he is speaking prophetically of Eve as his mother: "Eve became the mother of all who live" (Gen 3:20). If he was brought into being in sin, it does not follow that he himself is in sin, still less that he himself is sin.

Is everyone who turns from sin to faith, turning from sinful practices, as if from his mother, to life? I shall call in evidence one of the twelve prophets who says, "Am I to make an offering of my firstborn son for impiety, the fruit of my womb for the sin of my soul?" (Mic 6:7) This is no attack on the words "Increase in numbers" (Gen 1:28). He is calling the first impulses after birth, which do not help us to knowledge of God, "impiety." If anyone uses this as a basis for saying that that birth is evil, he should also use it as a basis for saying that it is good, in that in it we come to know the truth. "Come back to a sober and upright life and stop sinning. There are some who know nothing of God"—plainly the sinners (1 Cor 15:34). "Since we are not wrestling against flesh and blood, but against spiritual beings, potent in temptation, the rulers of this dark world," there is forbearance (Eph 6:12). This is why Paul says, "I bruise my own body and treat it as a slave" because "every athlete goes into total training" (instead of "total training" we understand not that he abstains from absolutely everything but that he shows self-control in those things he has taken a deliberate decision to use). "They do it to win a crown which dies, we for one which never dies," if we win the contest (1 Cor 9:25–27). No effort, no crown! Today there are some people who place the widow above the virgin in self-control, on the grounds that she has shown a high-minded rejection of a pleasure she has enjoyed.

If birth is an evil, then the blasphemers must place the Lord who went through birth and the virgin who gave him birth in the category of evil. Abominable people! In attacking birth they are maligning the will of God and the mystery of creation. This is the basis of Cassian's docetism, Marcion's too, yes, and Valentinus' "semi-spiritual body." It leads them to say, "Humanity became like cattle in coming to sexual intercourse." But it is when a man, swollen with lust, really and truly wants to go to bed with a woman not his own, that that sort of man actually becomes a wild beast. "They turned into stallions crazed for mares, each was whinnying for his neighbor's wife" (Jer 5:8). And if it is really argued that the snake took the practice of sexual union from the irrational animals, and prevailed on Adam to come to an agreement on sexual intercourse with Eve, and that the first created humans did not naturally practice this, this is another attack on creation for having made human beings weaker than the irrational beasts by nature, so that the people first created by God had to follow their example!

But if it was nature that guided them, like the animals without reason, to the production of children, and they were sexually aroused before they should have been, while they were still new and young because they were deceived and led astray, then God's judgment upon those who did not wait for his will was a just judgment. At the same time, birth is holy. It was through birth that the universe was constituted; so too the substances, the creatures, the angels, the powers, the souls, the commandment, the Law, the gospel, the revealed knowledge of God. And "all flesh is grass and all human glory is like the flower of grass. The grass dries up. The flower droops. But the Lord's word remains firm" (Is 40:6–8) and anoints the soul and makes it one with the Spirit. Without the body, how could dispensation for us, the Church, achieve its end? It was here that he, the Church's head (Eph 5:23), came in the flesh but without beauty of form, teaching us to fix our gaze on the formless incorporeality of the divine cause. "A tree of life," says the prophet, "grows in the soil of a healthy desire" (Prov 13:12), teaching that desires held in the living Lord are good and pure.

They now want that union of man and wife within marriage, which Scripture calls knowledge (Gen 2:9), to be a sin. They claim that this is indicated by the eating from the tree of good and evil, and teaches the fact that the commandment was transgressed by the use of the phrase "he knew." If so, then the revealed knowledge of the truth is also an eating from the Tree of Life. So it is possible for responsible marriage to take from that tree. We have previously said that it is possible to use marriage for good or evil, and this, if we do not transgress the commandment, is the tree of knowledge. Well? Does not the Savior heal body and soul alike from passions? It could not be, if the flesh were at enmity with the soul, that he would have put up fortifications against the soul in the soul's own territory by strengthening flesh, the enemy, with health. "Brothers, I tell you that flesh and blood are not able to inherit the kingdom of God; the perishable will never inherit imperishability" (1 Cor 15:50). For sin, being perishable, cannot enjoy fellowship with imperishability (that is righteousness). "Are you such fools?" he asks. "You have made a start with the Spirit. Are you now going to reach perfection through the flesh?" (Gal 3:3).

So there are some people who have tried to extend the scope of righteousness and the strong, sacred concord with the power of salvation, as we have demonstrated. They have a blasphemous acceptance of self-control combined with total atheism. It is proper to choose celibacy in accordance with the norm of health and to combine it with piety, in gratitude for God's gift of grace, without hatred of creation or denigration of married people. The universe is the product of creation; celibacy is the product of creation. Both should be grateful for their appointed condition, if they know what that is. But there are some who have kicked over the traces and run riot. They really are "stallions crazed for mares, whinnying for their neighbors' wives" (Jer 5:8). They cling uncontrollably to pleasure. They persuade their neighbors to hedonism. The miserable wretches listen to these words from Scripture: "Throw your lot in with us. Let us all have a common purse and a single bag for money" (Prov 1:14).

It is because of them that the same prophet gives us advice in these words: "Do not travel on the road with them; keep your steps clear of the paths they tread. It is not unjust for nets to be spread out for birds. By sharing in bloodshed they are laying up evils for themselves" (Prov 1:15–18)—that is to say, they are eager in pursuing immorality and are teaching their neighbors to do the same. "They are warriors," says the prophet, "beaten with their own tails"—or, as the Greeks put it, penises. Those to whom the prophecy alludes might well be lecherous, undisciplined fighters using their tails, children of darkness, "children of wrath," bloody assassins and murderers of their neighbors. "Clean away the old leaven to become bread of a fresh baking," the Apostle calls loudly to us (1 Cor 5:7). And again, in indignation at people like that, he instructs that "if any professed Christian practices fornication, is governed by the hope of profit, worships idols, uses abusive language, gets drunk, or is a swindler, we should have no fellowship, not even at table, with him" (1 Cor 5:11). "Through the Law," he says, "I am dead to the Law in order to live to God. I am crucified with Christ. It is no longer I who am alive"—in the way I used to live, lustfully—"but Christ who is alive in me," making me blessedly pure through obedience to the commandments. In consequence, whereas previously I was alive in the flesh following the ways of the flesh, "now my life in the flesh is lived by faith in God's Son" (Gal 2:19–20).

"Do not go off the road to gentile territory or visit a Samaritan town," says the Lord, to divert us from the opposite way of living, since "the lawless come to a dreadful fate. These are the paths of all those who achieve lawlessness" (Prov 1:18–19). "Alas for that man," says the Lord. "It was good for him never to have been born rather than cause one of my elect to stumble. Better for him to have a millstone tied around his neck and be drowned in the sea rather than misdirect one of my elect" (Mt 26:24). "God's name is dishonored because of them" (Rom 2:24). This is why the Apostle makes the lofty statement, "I wrote in my letter that you should have nothing to do with profligate living" down to "The body is not for sexual promiscuity but for the Lord, and the Lord for the body" (1 Cor 5:9–6:13). To make sure that he is not identifying marriage with fornication he adds, "Or do you not realize that anyone who attaches himself to a prostitute becomes physically one with her?" Will anyone call a virgin before marriage a prostitute? "Do not deprive one another," he says, "except temporarily by mutual agreement" (1 Cor 7:5). By using the word "deprive" he is showing the due obligation of marrying, the production of children. He made a point of this earlier in the words, "The husband must give the wife what is her due, and *vice versa*" (1 Cor 7:3).

After making this contribution, she is a helpmate domestically and in the Christian faith. He goes on to speak more clearly: "I have an order for the married. It is not from me but from the Lord. A wife is not to seek separation from her husband. If she does, she is to remain unmarried or come to reconciliation with her husband. The husband is not to divorce his wife. To the rest I speak in my own person not as representing the Lord. If any Christian male" down to "but now they are dedicated to God" (1 Cor 7:10–14). These people who run down the Law and marriage as if it were constituted merely by the Law and alien to the New Covenant—what do they say in face of this? Those who have such a loathing for sex and childbirth—what have they to say in answer to this legislation? For Paul also lays down that leadership in the Church should rest with "a bishop who presides successfully over his household" and that "marriage to one wife" constitutes a household with the Lord's blessing (1 Tim 3:2–4; Tit 1:6).

"So to the pure, everything is pure," he says. "To the tainted minds of the faithless, nothing is pure; they are tainted in reason and conscience" (Tit 1:15). As to illegitimate pleasure he says, "Make no mistake. The sexually immoral, worshippers of idols, adulterers, passive perverts, homosexuals, those who pursue profit, robbers, drunkards, people who use abusive language, and swindlers will not inherit the kingdom of God." We used to be such, but "have passed through the purifying waters" (1 Cor 6:9–11). But they purify themselves for this licentiousness. Their baptism is out of responsible self-control into sexual immorality. Their philosophy is the gratification of their pleasures and passions. They teach a change from self-discipline to indiscipline. The hope they offer is the titillation of their genitals. They make themselves excluded from the kingdom of God instead of enrolled disciples. Under the name of what they falsely call knowledge they have embarked on the road to outer darkness. "For the rest, brothers, set your minds on all that is true, all that is holy, all that is righteous, all that is pure, all that is attractive, all that wins praise, whatever wins admiration for its moral excellence. Put into practice the lessons I taught, the traditions I passed on, the words you heard from me, the actions you saw me perform. And the God of Peace will be with you" (Phil 4:8–9).

Peter in his letter says much the same: "In consequence, you have purified your souls in obedience to the truth, and your faith and hope are in God" (1 Pet 1:21–22), "as obedient children, not molded by the lustful desires of your former ignorance. The one who called you is holy. Be like him, holy in all your behavior, since it is written, 'You are to be holy, since I am holy'" (1 Pet 1:14–16). But our critique of the hypocritical pretenders to knowledge, however essential, has gone beyond what is necessary and stretched out our discourse to a considerable length. So this is the conclusion of Book Three of our *Miscellanies of Notes of Revealed Knowledge in Accordance with the True Philosophy.*

1. Describe the scriptural arguments that Clement employs against the Gnostic despisers of marriage.
2. Why is self-discipline important for Clement?
3. What does Clement think of celibacy?

Tertullian

Born in Carthage, North Africa, the son of a soldier, Tertullian (c. 160–c. 220) became a well-known lawyer in Rome. In his thirties, he converted to Christianity. A married man, he wrote numerous significant theological treatises before breaking with the Catholic Church over concern about the Church's supposed moral laxity. Before he fell into this rigorism, he wrote the treatise addressed to his wife that is excerpted below. After warning against second marriage on the grounds that the second partner might drag down his wife into a licentious lifestyle, he describes the equality of husband and wife in Christian marriage, and emphasizes their mutual assistance on the path to eternal life.

THE HANDMAID OF GOD DWELLS amid alien labors; and among these labors, on all the memorial days of demons, at all solemnities of kings, at the beginning of the year, at the beginning of the month, she will be agitated by the odor of incense. And she will have to go forth from her house by a gate wreathed with laurel, and hung with lanterns, as from some new consistory of public lusts; she will have to sit with her husband often in club meetings, often in taverns; and, used as she was formerly to minister to the "saints," will sometimes have to minister to the "unjust." And will she not hence recognize a prejudgment of her own

From "To His Wife," trans. H. Ellershaw, in *Nicene and Post-Nicene Fathers*, ed. Alexander Roberts and James Donaldson, vol. 4, *Tertullian, Part Fourth; Minicius Felix; Commodian; Origen, Parts First and Second* (Peabody, Mass.: Hendrickson, 1994 [1885]), 47–49.

damnation, in that she *tends* them whom formerly she was expecting to *judge*? whose hand will she yearn after? of whose cup will she partake? What will her husband sing to her, or she to her husband? From the tavern, I suppose, she who sups upon God will hear somewhat! From hell what mention of God arises? What invocation of Christ? Where are the fosterings of faith by the interspersion of the Scriptures in conversation? where the Spirit? where refreshment? where the divine benediction? All things strange, all inimical, all condemned; aimed by the Evil One for the attrition of salvation!

If these things may happen to those women also who, having attained the faith while in the state of Gentile matrimony, continue in that state, still they are excused, as having been "apprehended by God" (Phil 3:12) in these very circumstances; and they are bidden to persevere in their married state, and are sanctified, and have hope of "making a gain" held out to them. "If, then, a marriage of this kind contracted *before* conversion stands ratified before God, why should not one contracted *after* conversion too go prosperously forward, so as not to be thus harassed by pressures, and straits, and hindrances, and defilements, having already as it has the partial sanction of divine grace?" Because, on the one hand, the wife in the former case, called *from among* the Gentiles to the exercise of some eminent heavenly virtue, is, by the visible proofs of some marked divine regard, a terror to her Gentile husband, so as to make him less ready to annoy her, less active in laying snares for her, less diligent in playing the spy over her. He has felt "mighty works"; he has seen experimental evidences; he knows her changed for the better: thus even he himself is, by his fear, a candidate for God. Thus men of this kind, with regard to whom the grace of God has established a familiar intimacy, are more easily "gained." But, on the other hand, to descend into forbidden ground unsolicited and spontaneously, is quite another thing. Things which are not pleasing to the Lord, of course offend the Lord, are of course introduced by the Evil One. A sign hereof is the fact, that it is *wooers* only who find the Christian name pleasing; and, accordingly, some heathen men are found not to shrink in horror from Christian women, just in order to exterminate them, to wrest them away, to exclude them from the faith. So long as marriage of this kind is procured by the Evil One, but condemned by God, you have a reason why you need not doubt that it can in no case be carried to a prosperous end.

Let us further inquire, as if we were in very deed inquisitors of divine sentences, whether they be lawfully thus condemned. Even among the nations, do not all the strictest lords and most tenacious of discipline interdict their own slaves from marrying out of their own house?—in order, of course, that they may not run into lascivious excess, desert their duties, purvey their lords' goods to strangers. Yet, further, have not the nations decided that such women as have, after their lords' formal warning, persisted in intercourse with other men's slaves, may be claimed as slaves? Shall earthly disciplines be held more strict than heavenly prescripts; so that *Gentile* women, if united to strangers, lose their liberty; *ours* conjoin to themselves the devil's slaves, and continue in their former position? Forsooth, they will deny that any formal warning has been given them by the Lord through His own apostle!

What am I to fasten on as the cause of this madness, except the weakness of faith, ever prone to the concupiscences of worldly joys?—which, indeed, is chiefly found among the wealthier; for the more any is rich, and inflated with the name of "matron," the more capacious house does she require for her burdens, as it were a field wherein ambition may run its course. To such the churches look paltry. A rich man is a difficult thing to find in the house of God; and if such a one is found there, difficult is it to find such unmarried. What, then, are they to do? Whence but from the devil are they to seek a husband apt for maintaining their sedan, and their mules, and their hair-curlers of outlandish stature? A Christian, even although rich, would perhaps not afford all these. Set before yourself, I beg of you, the examples of the Gentiles. Most Gentile women, noble in extraction and wealthy in property, unite themselves indiscriminately with the ignoble and the mean, sought out for themselves for luxurious, or mutilated for licentious, purposes. Some take up with their own freedmen and slaves, despising public opinion, provided they may but have husbands from whom to fear no impediment to their own liberty. To a Christian believer it is irksome to wed a believer inferior to herself in estate, destined as she will be to have her wealth augmented in the person of a poor husband! For if it is "the poor," not the rich, "whose are the kingdoms of the heavens," the rich will find more in the poor than she brings him, or than she would in the rich. She will be dowered with an ampler dowry from the goods of him who is rich in God. Let her be on an equality with him on earth, who in the heavens will perhaps not be so. Is there need for doubt, and inquiry, and repeated deliberation, whether he whom God has entrusted with His own property is fit for dotal endowments? Whence are we to find words enough fully to tell the happiness of that marriage which the Church cements, and the oblation confirms, and the benediction signs and seals; which angels carry back the news of to heaven, which the Father holds for ratified? For even on earth children do not rightly and lawfully wed without their fathers' consent. What kind of yoke is that of two believers, partakers of one hope, one desire, one discipline, one and the same service? Both are brethren, both fellow servants, no difference of spirit or flesh; nay, they are truly "two in one flesh" (Gen 2:24). Where the flesh is one, one is the spirit too. Together they pray, together prostrate themselves, together perform their fasts; mutually teaching, mutually exhorting, mutually sustaining. Equally are they both found in the Church of God; equally at the banquet of God; equally in straits, in persecutions, in refreshments. Neither hides aught from the other; neither shuns the other; neither is troublesome to the other. The sick are visited, the indigent relieved, with freedom. Alms are given without danger of ensuing torment; sacrifices attended without scruple; daily diligence discharged without impediment: there is no stealthy signing, no trembling greeting, no mute benediction. Between the two echo psalms and hymns; and they mutually challenge each other which shall better chant to their Lord. Such things when Christ sees and hears, He joys. To these He sends His own peace. Where two are, there withal is He Himself. Where He is, there the Evil One is not.

These are the things which that utterance of the apostle has, beneath its brevity, left to be understood by us. These things, if need shall be, suggest to your own mind. By these turn yourself away from the examples of some. To marry *otherwise* is, to believers, not "lawful"; is not "expedient."

1. How does Tertullian describe the relationship between a Christian husband and wife?
2. Why does he warn against remarriage?

St. Gregory of Nazianzus

St. Gregory of Nazianzus (c. 330–c. 390) was a fellow student with St. Basil as a young man at Caesarea and later at Athens, and became a friend both of Basil and of St. Gregory of Nyssa. In a lifetime of service to the Church, he composed various theological treatises, letters, poems, and sermons. This excerpt from his eulogy for his sister evinces his understanding of marriage, in which the partners, distinct in body but equal in soul, are measured by their holiness of life. He comments as well upon the worthiness of his parents, Gregory and Nonna, arguing that his father, a bishop in a time of married clergy, learned how to be a "good shepherd" from his wife.

IN PRAISING MY SISTER, I shall pay honor to one of my own family; yet my praise will not be false, because it is given to a relation, but, because it is true, will be worthy of commendation, and its truth is based not only upon its justice, but upon well-known facts. For, even if I wished, I should not be permitted to be partial; since everyone who hears me stands, like a skilful critic, between my oration and the truth, to discountenance exaggeration, yet, if he be a man of justice, demanding what is really due. So that my fear is not of outrunning the truth,

From "Funeral Oration on His Sister Gorgonia," trans. Charles Gordon Browne and James Edward Swallow, in *Nicene and Post-Nicene Fathers*, second series, ed. Philip Schaff and Henry Wace, vol. 7, *Cyril of Jerusalem, Gregory Nazianzen* (Peabody, Mass.: Hendrickson, 1995 [1894]), 238–242, 244.

but, on the contrary, of falling short of it, and lessening her just repute by the extreme inadequacy of my panegyric; for it is a hard task to match her excellences with suitable action and words. Let us not then be so unjust as to praise every characteristic of other folk, and disparage really valuable qualities because they are our own, so as to make some men gain by their absence of kindred with us, while others suffer for their relationship. For justice would be violated alike by the praise of the one and the neglect of the other, whereas if we make the truth our standard and rule, and look to her alone, disregarding all the objects of the vulgar and the mean, we shall praise or pass over everything according to its merits.

Yet it would be most unreasonable of all, if, while we refuse to regard it as a righteous thing to defraud, insult, accuse, or treat unjustly in any way, great or small, those who are our kindred, and consider wrong done to those nearest to us the worst of all, we were yet to imagine that it would be an act of justice to deprive them of such an oration as is due most of all to the good, and spend more words upon those who are evil, and beg for indulgent treatment, than on those who are excellent and merely claim their due. For if we are not prevented, as would be far more just, from praising men who have lived outside our own circle, because we do not know and cannot personally testify to their merits, shall we be prevented from praising those whom we do know, because of our friendship, or the envy of the multitude, and especially those who have departed hence, whom it is too late to ingratiate ourselves with, since they have escaped, amongst all other things, from the reach of praise or blame.

Having now made a sufficient defense on these points, and shown how necessary it is for me to be the speaker, come, let me proceed with my eulogy, rejecting all daintiness and elegance of style (for she whom we are praising was unadorned and the absence of ornament was to her, beauty), and yet performing, as a most indispensable debt, all those funeral rites which are her due, and further instructing everyone in a zealous imitation of the same virtue, since it is my object in every word and action to promote the perfection of those committed to my charge. The task of praising the country and family of our departed one I leave to another, more scrupulous in adhering to the rules of eulogy; not will he lack many fair topics, if he wish to deck her with external ornaments, as men deck a splendid and beautiful form with gold and precious stones, and the artistic devices of the craftsman; which, while they accentuate ugliness by their contrast, can add no attractiveness to the beauty which surpasses them. For my part, I will only conform to such rules so far as to allude to our common parents, for it would not be reverent to pass unnoticed the great blessing of having such parents and teachers, and then speedily direct my attention to herself, without further taxing the patience of those who are eager to learn what manner of woman she was.

Who is there who knows not the Abraham and Sarah of these our latter days, Gregory and Nonna his wife? For it is not well to omit the incitement to virtue of mentioning their names. He has been justified by faith, she has dwelt with him who is faithful; he beyond all hope has been the father of many nations, she has spiritually travailed in their birth; he escaped from the bondage of his father's gods, she is the daughter as well as the mother of the free; he went out from kindred and home for the sake of the land of promise, she was the occasion of his exile; for on this head alone I venture to claim for her an honor higher than that of Sarah; he set forth on so noble a pilgrimage, she readily shared with him in its toils; he gave himself to the Lord, she both called her husband lord and regarded him as such, and in part was thereby justified; whose was the promise, from whom, as far as in them lay, was born Isaac, and whose was the gift.

This good shepherd was the result of his wife's prayers and guidance, and it was from her that he learned his ideal of a good shepherd's life. He generously fled from his idols, and afterwards even put demons to flight; he never consented to eat salt with idolators: united together with a bond of one honor, of one mind, of one soul, concerned as much with virtue and fellowship with God as with the flesh; equal in length of life and hoary hairs, equal in prudence and brilliancy, rivals of each other, soaring beyond all the rest, possessed in few respects by the flesh, and translated in spirit, even before dissolution: possessing not the world, and yet possessing it, by at once despising and rightly valuing it: forsaking riches and yet being rich through their noble pursuits; rejecting things here, and purchasing instead the things yonder: possessed of a scanty remnant of this life, left over from their piety, but of an abundant and long life for which they have labored. I will say but one word more about them: they have been rightly and fairly assigned, each to either sex; he is the ornament of men, she of women, and not only the ornament but the pattern of virtue.

From them Gorgonia derived both her existence and her reputation; they sowed in her the seeds of piety, they were the source of her fair life, and of her happy departure with better hopes. Fair privileges these, and such as are not easily attained by many of those who plume themselves highly upon their noble birth, and are proud of their ancestry. But, if I must treat of her case in a more philosophic and lofty strain, Gorgonia's native land was Jerusalem above, the object, not of sight but of contemplation, wherein is our commonwealth, and whereto we are pressing on: whose citizen Christ is, and whose fellow-citizens are the assembly and church of the firstborn who are written in heaven, and feast around its great Founder in contemplation of His glory, and take part in the endless festival; her nobility consisted in the preservation of the Image, and the perfect likeness to the Archetype, which is produced by reason and virtue and pure desire, ever more and more conforming, in things pertaining to God, to those truly initiated into the heavenly mysteries; and in knowing whence, and of what character, and for what end we came into being.

This is what I know upon these points: and therefore it is that I both am aware and assert that her soul was more noble than those of the East, according to a better than the ordinary rule of noble or ignoble birth, whose distinctions depend not on blood but on character; nor does it classify those whom it praises or blames according to their families, but as individuals. But speaking as I do of her excellences among those who know her, let each one join in contributing some particular and aid me in my speech: for it is impossible for one man to take in every point, however gifted with observation and intelligence.

In modesty she so greatly excelled, and so far surpassed, those of her own day, to say nothing of those of old time who have been illustrious for modesty, that, in regard to the two divisions of the life of all, that is, the married and the unmarried state, the latter being higher and more divine, though more difficult and dangerous, while the former is more humble and more safe, she was able to avoid the disadvantages of each, and to select and combine all that is best in both, namely, the elevation of the one and the security of the other, thus becoming modest without pride, blending the excellence of the married with that of the unmarried state, and proving that neither of them absolutely binds us to, or separates us from, God or the world (so that the one from its own nature must be utterly avoided, and the other altogether praised): but that it is mind which nobly presides over wedlock and maidenhood, and arranges and works upon them as the raw material of virtue under the master-hand of reason. For though she had entered upon a carnal union, she was not therefore separated from the spirit, nor, because her husband was her head, did she ignore her first Head: but, performing those few ministrations due to the world and nature, according to the will of the law of the flesh, or rather of Him who gave to the flesh these laws, she consecrated herself entirely to God. But what is most excellent and honorable, she also won over her husband to her side, and made of him a good fellow-servant, instead of an unreasonable master. And not only so, but she further made the fruit of her body, her children and her children's children, to be the fruit of her spirit, dedicating to God not her single soul, but the whole family and household, and making wedlock illustrious through her own acceptability in wedlock, and the fair harvest she had reaped thereby; presenting herself, as long as she lived, as an example to her offspring of all that was good, and when summoned hence, leaving her will behind her, as a silent exhortation to her house.

The divine Solomon, in his instructive wisdom, I mean his Proverbs, praises the woman who looks to her household and loves her husband (Prov 31), contrasting her with one who roams abroad, and is uncontrolled and dishonorable, and hunts for precious souls with wanton words and ways, while she manages well at home and bravely sets about her woman's duties, as her hands hold the distaff, and she prepares two coats for her husband, buying a field in due season, and makes good provision for the food of her servants, and welcomes her friends at a liberal table; with all the other details in which he sings the praises of the modest and industrious woman. Now, to praise my sister in these points would be to praise a statue for its shadow, or a lion for its claws, without allusion to its greatest perfections. Who was more deserving of renown, and yet who avoided it so much and made herself inaccessible to the eyes of man? Who knew better the due proportions of sobriety and cheerfulness, so that her sobriety should not seem inhuman, nor her tenderness immodest, but prudent in one, gentle in the other, her discretion was marked by a combination of sympathy and dignity? Listen, you women addicted to ease and display, who despise the veil of shamefastness. Who ever so kept her eyes under control? Who so derided laughter, that the ripple of a smile seemed a great thing to her? Who more steadfastly closed her ears? And who opened them more to the Divine words, or rather, who installed the mind as ruler of the tongue in uttering the judgments of God? Who, as she, regulated her lips?

Here, if you will, is another point of her excellence: one of which neither she nor any truly modest and decorous woman thinks anything: but which we have been made to think much of, by those who are too fond of ornament and display, and refuse to listen to instruction on such matters. She was never adorned with gold wrought into artistic forms of surpassing beauty, nor flaxen tresses, fully or partially displayed, nor spiral curls, nor dishonoring designs of men who construct erections on the honorable head, nor costly folds of flowing and transparent robes, nor graces of brilliant stones, which color the neighboring air, and cast a glow upon the form; nor the arts and witcheries of the painter, nor that cheap beauty of the infernal creator who works against the Divine, hiding with his treacherous pigments the creation of God, and putting it to shame with his honor, and setting before eager eyes the imitation of a harlot instead of the form of God, so that this bastard beauty may steal away that image which should be kept for God and for the world to come. But though she was aware of the many and various external ornaments of women, yet none of them was more precious to her than her own character, and the brilliancy stored up within. One red tint was dear to her, the blush of modesty; one white one, the sign of temperance: but pigments and pencilings, and living pictures, and flowing lines of beauty, she left to women of the stage and of the streets, and to all who think it a shame and a reproach to be ashamed.

Enough of such topics. Of her prudence and piety no adequate account can be given, nor many examples found besides those of her natural and spiritual parents, who were her only models, and of whose virtue she in no wise fell short, with this single exception most readily admitted, that they, as she both knew and acknowledged, were the source of her goodness, and the root of her own illumination. What could be keener than the intellect of her who was recognized as a common adviser not only by those of her family, those of the same people and of the one fold, but even by all men round about, who treated her counsels and advice as a law not to be broken? What more sagacious than her words? What more prudent than her silence? Having mentioned silence, I will proceed to that which was most characteristic of her, most becoming to women, and most serviceable to these times. Who had a fuller knowledge of the things of God, both from the Divine oracles, and from her own understanding? But who was less ready to speak, confining herself within the due limits of women? Moreover, as was the bounden duty of a woman who has learned true piety, and that which is the only honorable object of insatiate desire, who, as she, adorned temples with offerings, both others and this one, which will hardly, now she is gone, be so adorned again? Or rather, who so presented herself to God as a living temple? Who again paid such honor to priests, especially to him who was her fellow soldier and teacher of piety, whose are the good seeds, and the pair of children consecrated to God?

Who opened her house to those who live according to God with a more graceful and bountiful welcome? And, which is greater than this, who bade them welcome with such modesty and godly greetings? Further, who showed a mind more unmoved in sufferings? Whose soul was more sympathetic to those in trouble? Whose hand more liberal to those in want? I should not hesitate to honor her with the words of Job: Her door was opened to all comers; the stranger did not lodge in the street. She was eyes to the blind, feet to the lame, a mother to the orphan (Job 31:32; 29:15). Why should I say more of her compassion to widows, than that its fruit which she obtained was, never to be called a widow herself? Her house was a common abode to all the needy of her family; and her goods no less common to all in need than their own belonged to each. She hath dispersed abroad and given to the poor (Ps 112:9), and according to the infallible truth of the Gospel, she laid up much store in the winepresses above, and oftentimes entertained Christ in the person of those whose benefactress she was. And, best of all, there was in her no unreal profession, but in secret she cultivated piety before Him who seeth secret things. Everything she rescued from the ruler of this world, everything she transferred to the safe garners. Nothing did she leave behind to earth, save her body. She bartered everything for the hopes above: the sole wealth she left to her children was the imitation of her example, and emulation of her merits.

But amid these tokens of incredible magnanimity, she did not surrender her body to luxury, and unrestrained pleasures of the appetite, that raging and tearing dog, as though presuming upon her acts of benevolence, as most men do, who redeem their luxury by compassion to the poor, and instead of healing evil with good, receive evil as a recompense for their good deeds. Nor did she, while subduing her dust by fasting, leave to another the medicine of hard lying; nor, while she found this of spiritual service, was she less restrained in sleep than anyone else; nor, while regulating her life on this point as if freed from the body, did she lie upon the ground, when others were passing the night erect, as the most mortified men struggle to do. Nay in this respect she was seen to surpass not only women, but the most devoted of men, by her intelligent chanting of the psalter, her converse with, and unfolding and apposite recollection of, the Divine oracles, her bending of her knees which had grown hard and almost taken root in the ground, her tears to cleanse her stains with contrite heart and spirit of lowliness, her prayer rising heavenward, her mind freed from wandering in rapture; in all these, or in any one of them, is there man or woman who can boast of having surpassed her? Besides, it is a great thing to say, but it is true, that while she was zealous in her endeavor after some points of excellence, of others she was the paragon: of some she was the discoverer, in others she excelled. And if in some single particular she was rivaled, her superiority consists in her complete grasp of all. Such was her success in all points, as none else attained even in a moderate degree in one: to such perfection did she attain in each particular, that any one might of itself have supplied the place of all.

O untended body, and squalid garments, whose only flower is virtue! O soul, clinging to the body, when reduced almost to an immaterial state through lack of food; or rather, when the body had been mortified by force, even before dissolution, that the soul might attain to freedom, and escape the entanglements of the senses! O nights of vigil, and psalmody, and standing which lasts from one day to another! O David, whose strains never seem tedious to faithful souls! O tender limbs, flung upon the earth and, contrary to nature, growing hard! O fountains of tears, sowing in affliction that they might reap in joy. O cry in the night, piercing the clouds and reaching unto Him that dwelleth in the heavens! O fervor of spirit, waxing bold in prayerful longings against the dogs of night, and frosts and rain, and thunders, and hail, and darkness! O nature of woman overcoming that of man in the common struggle for salvation, and demonstrating that the distinction between male and female is one of body not of soul! O Baptismal purity, O soul, in the pure chamber of thy body, the bride of Christ! O bitter eating! O Eve mother of our race and of our sin! O subtle serpent, and death, overcome by her self-discipline! O self-emptying of Christ, and form of a servant, and sufferings, honored by her mortification!

[. . .]

She had recently obtained the blessing of cleansing and perfection, which we have all received from God as a common gift and foundation of our *new* life. Or rather all her life was a cleansing and perfecting: and while she received regeneration from the Holy Spirit, its security was hers by virtue of her former life. And in her case almost alone, I will venture to say, the mystery was a seal rather than a gift of grace. And when her husband's perfection was her one remaining desire (and if you wish me briefly to describe the man, I do not know what more to say of him than that he was her husband) in order that she might be consecrated to God in her whole body, and not depart half-perfected, or leave behind her imperfect anything that was hers; she did not even fail of this petition, from Him Who fulfills the desire of them that fear Him, and accomplishes their requests.

And now when she had all things to her mind, and nothing was lacking of her desires, and the appointed time drew nigh, being thus prepared for death and departure, she fulfilled the law which prevails in such matters, and took to her bed. After many injunctions to her husband, her children, and her friends, as was to be expected from one who was full of conjugal, maternal, and brotherly love, and after making her last day a day of solemn festival with brilliant discourse upon the things above, she fell asleep, full not of the days of man, for which she had no desire, knowing them to be evil for her, and mainly occupied with our dust and wanderings, but more exceedingly full of the days of God, than I imagine any one even of those who have departed in a wealth of hoary hairs, and have numbered many terms of years. Thus she was set free, or, it is better to say, taken to God, or flew away, or changed her abode, or anticipated by a little the departure of her body.

1. What does Gregory say about his parents?
2. What, according to Gregory, are the characteristics that marked his sister as an exemplary wife to her husband?

St. Gregory of Nyssa

St. Gregory of Nyssa (335–394), brother of St. Basil the Great, belonged to a marvelous Christian family: his father, two brothers, and sister are venerated as saints. After the death of his wife, he entered a monastery, and in his thirties he became bishop of Nyssa. In the following passage from his treatise *On Virginity* he seeks to propose an understanding of consecrated celibacy that, while respecting the goodness of marriage, nonetheless acknowledges the particular strengths of the celibate path. The Fathers' praise of celibacy has often led to accusations that they deprecated marriage, but in fact, as Gregory of Nyssa points out, most people have experience of marriage but find consecrated virginity off-putting. Gregory suggests that a proper understanding of consecrated virginity assists married couples in recognizing that their own vocation, too, has sanctification as its goal, rather than merely worldly pleasures.

A N ILLUSTRATION WILL MAKE OUR TEACHING on this subject clearer. Imagine a stream flowing from a spring and dividing itself off into a number of accidental channels. As long as it proceeds so, it will be useless for any purpose of agriculture, the dissipation of its waters making each particular current small and feeble, and therefore slow. But if one were to mass these wandering and widely dispersed rivulets again into

From "On Virginity," trans. William Moore and Henry Austin Wilson, in *Nicene and Post-Nicene Fathers*, second series, ed. Philip Schaff and Henry Wace, vol. 5, *Gregory of Nyssa: Dogmatic Treatises, Etc.* (Peabody, Mass.: Hendrickson, 1995 [1892]), 352–353.

one single channel, he would have a full and collected stream for the
supplies which life demands. Just so the human mind (so it seems to
me), as long as its current spreads itself in all directions over the pleasures of the sense, has no power that is worth the naming of making its
way towards the Real Good; but once call it back and collect it upon itself, so that it may begin to move without scattering and wandering towards the activity which is congenital and natural to it, it will find no
obstacle in mounting to higher things, and in grasping realities. We
often see water contained in a pipe bursting upwards through this con-
straining force, which will not let it leak; and this, in spite of its natural
gravitation: in the same way, the mind of man, enclosed in the compact
channel of a habitual continence, and not having any side issues, will be
raised by virtue of its natural powers of motion to an exalted love. In
fact, its Maker ordained that it should always move, and to stop is impossible to it; when therefore it is prevented employing this power upon
trifles, it cannot be but that it will speed toward the truth, all improper
exits being closed. In the case of many turnings we see travellers can
keep to the direct route, when they have learnt that the other roads are
wrong, and so avoid them; the more they keep out of these wrong directions, the more they will preserve the straight course; in like manner
the mind in turning from vanities will recognize the truth. The great
prophets, then, whom we have mentioned seem to teach this lesson, viz.
to entangle ourselves with none of the objects of this world's effort; marriage is one of these, or rather it is the primal root of all striving after
vanities.

Let no one think however that herein we depreciate marriage as an institution. We are well aware that it is not a stranger to God's blessing. But
since the common instincts of mankind can plead sufficiently on its behalf, instincts which prompt by a spontaneous bias to take the high road
of marriage for the procreation of children, whereas Virginity in a way
thwarts this natural impulse, it is a superfluous task to compose for-
mally an Exhortation to marriage. We put forward the pleasure of it instead, as a most doughty champion on its behalf. It may be however,
notwithstanding this, that there *is* some need of such a treatise, occa-
sioned by those who travesty the teaching of the Church. Such persons
"have their conscience seared with a hot iron" (1 Tim 4:2), as the Apostle expresses it; and very truly too, considering that, deserting the guidance of the Holy Spirit for the "doctrines of devils," they have some ul-

cers and blisters stamped upon their hearts, abominating God's creatures, and calling them "foul," "seducing," "mischievous," and so on. "But
what have I to do to judge them that are without?" asks the Apostle (1
Cor 5:12). Truly those persons are outside the Court in which the words
of our mysteries are spoken; they are not installed under God's roof, but
in the monastery of the Evil One. They "are taken captive by him at his
will" (2 Tim 2:16).

They therefore do not understand that all virtue is found in moderation, and that any declension to either side of it becomes a vice. He, in
fact, who grasps the middle point between doing too little and doing too
much has hit the distinction between vice and virtue. Instances will
make this clearer. Cowardice and audacity are two recognized vices opposed to each other; the one the defect, the other the excess of confidence; between them lies courage. Again, piety is neither atheism nor
superstition; it is equally impious to deny a God and to believe in many
gods. Is there need of more examples to bring this principle home? The
man who avoids both meanness and prodigality will by this shunning of
extremes form the moral habit of liberality; for liberality is the thing
which is neither inclined to spend at random vast and useless sums, nor
yet to be closely calculating in necessary expenses.

We need not go into details in the case of all good qualities. Reason,
in all of them, has established virtue to be a middle state between two
extremes. Sobriety itself therefore is a middle state, and manifestly involves the two declensions on either side towards vice; he, that is, who is
wanting in firmness of soul, and is so easily worsted in the combat with
pleasure as never even to have approached the path of a virtuous and
sober life, slides into shameful indulgence; while he who goes beyond
the safe ground of sobriety and overshoots the moderation of this
virtue, falls as it were from a precipice into the "doctrines of devils,"
"having his conscience seared with a hot iron." In declaring marriage
abominable he brands himself with such reproaches; for "if the tree is
corrupt" (as the Gospel says [Mt 7:18]), "the fruit also of the tree will be
like it"; if a man is the shoot and fruitage of the tree of marriage, reproaches cast on that turn upon him who casts them. These persons,
then, are like branded criminals already; their conscience is covered with
the stripes of this unnatural teaching.

But our view of marriage is this; that, while the pursuit of heavenly
things should be a man's first care, yet if he can use the advantages of

marriage with sobriety and moderation, he need not despise this way of serving the state. An example might be found in the patriarch Isaac. He married Rebecca when he was past the flower of his age and his prime was well-nigh spent, so that his marriage was not the deed of passion, but because of God's blessing that should be upon his seed. He cohabited with her till the birth of her only children, and then, closing the channels of the senses, lived wholly for the Unseen; for this is what seems to be meant by the mention in his history of the *dimness* of the Patriarch's eyes. But let that be as those think who are skilled in reading these meanings, and let us proceed with the continuity of our discourse. What, then, were we saying? That in the cases where it is possible at once to be true to the diviner love, and to embrace wedlock, there is no reason for setting aside this dispensation of nature and misrepresenting as abominable that which is honourable.

Let us take again our illustration of the water and the spring. Whenever the husbandman, in order to irrigate a particular spot, is bringing the stream thither, but there is need before it gets there of a small outlet, he will allow only so much to escape into that outlet as is adequate to supply the demand, and can then easily be blended again with the main stream. If, as an inexperienced and easygoing steward, he opens too wide a channel, there will be danger of the whole stream quitting its direct bed and pouring itself sideways. In the same way, if (as life does need a mutual succession) a man so treats this need as to give spiritual things the first thought, and because of the shortness of the time indulges but sparingly the sexual passion and keeps it under restraint, that man would realize the character of the prudent husbandman to which the Apostle exhorts us. About the details of paying these trifling debts of nature he will not be over-calculating, but the long hours of his prayers will secure the purity which is the keynote of his life. He will always fear lest by this kind of indulgence he may become nothing but flesh and blood; for in them God's Spirit does not dwell.

He who is of so weak a character that he cannot make a manful stand against nature's impulse had better keep himself very far away from such temptations, rather than descend into a combat which is above his strength. There is no small danger for him lest, cajoled in the valuation of pleasure, he should think that there exists no other good but that which is enjoyed along with some sensual emotion, and, turning altogether from the love of immaterial delights, should become entirely of the flesh, seeking always his pleasure only there, so that his character will be a Pleasure-lover, not a God-lover. It is not every man's gift, owing to weakness of nature, to hit the due proportion in these matters; there is a danger of being carried far beyond it, and "sticking fast in the deep mire," to use the Psalmist's words (Ps 69:2). It would therefore be for our interest, as our discourse has been suggesting, to pass through life without a trial of these temptations, lest under cover of the excuse of lawful indulgence passion should gain an entrance into the citadel of the soul.

1. Is it possible to praise consecrated virginity without denigrating marriage?
2. How can marriage go wrong, according to Gregory?
3. Is marriage dishonorable in Gregory's view?

St. Augustine

Born in North Africa, St. Augustine (354–430) gave up a promising career as a rhetorician to devote himself to prayer and study after his conversion to Christianity in 387. Soon after his conversion, he returned to North Africa. His abilities were recognized and he was appointed bishop of Hippo in North Africa, where he served for the remainder of his life. The author of many of the greatest works of Christian theology—including *On the Trinity*, *The City of God*, *On Christian Doctrine*, and *Confessions*—he is known for his inquisitive and penetrating mind, and for his tireless writing and preaching. The following selection from his autobiographical *Confessions* describes his early life in his parents' home, his descent into disordered sexuality (greeted by his father as a welcome sign of virile "manhood"), and his mother's prayers for his conversion. Perhaps no one has depicted ancient family relationships more memorably than St. Augustine.

INTEND TO REMIND MYSELF of my past foulnesses and carnal corruptions, not because I love them but so that I may love you, my God. It is from love of your love that I make the act of recollection. The recalling of my wicked ways is bitter in my memory, but I do it so that you may be sweet to me, a sweetness touched by no deception, a sweetness serene and content. You gathered me together from the state of disintegration in which I had been fruitlessly divided. I turned from unity in you to be lost in multiplicity.

From *Confessions,* trans. Henry Chadwick (Oxford: Oxford University Press, 1991), 24–28, 49–51. By permission of Oxford University Press.

At one time in adolescence I was burning to find satisfaction in hell-ish pleasures. I ran wild in the shadowy jungle of erotic adventures. "My beauty wasted away and in your sight I became putrid" (Dan 10:8), by pleasing myself and by being ambitious to win human approval.

The single desire that dominated my search for delight was simply to love and to be loved. But no restraint was imposed by the exchange of mind with mind, which marks the brightly lit pathway of friend-ship. Clouds of muddy carnal concupiscence filled the air. The bub-bling impulses of puberty befogged and obscured my heart so that it could not see the difference between love's serenity and lust's darkness. Confusion of the two things boiled within me. It seized hold of my youthful weakness sweeping me through the precipitous rocks of de-sire to submerge me in a whirlpool of vice. Your wrath was heavy upon me and I was unaware of it. I had become deafened by the clanking chain of my mortal condition, the penalty of my pride. I travelled very far from you, and you did not stop me. I was tossed about and spilt, scattered and boiled dry in my fornications. And you were silent. How slow I was to find my joy! At that time you said nothing, and I travelled much further away from you into more and more sterile things pro-ductive of unhappiness, proud in my self-pity, incapable of rest in my exhaustion.

If only someone could have imposed restraint on my disorder. That would have transformed to good purpose the fleeting experiences of beauty in these lowest of things, and fixed limits to indulgence in their charms. Then the stormy waves of my youth would have finally broken on the shore of marriage. Even so, I could not have been wholly con-tent to confine sexual union to acts intended to procreate children, as your law prescribes, Lord. For you shape the propagation of our mor-tal race, imposing your gentle hand to soften the brambles which were excluded from your paradise. Your omnipotence is never far from us, even when we are far from you. Alternatively, I ought to have paid more vigilant heed to the voice from your clouds: "Nevertheless those who are married shall have trouble in the flesh, and I would spare you" (Cor 7:28), and "It is good for a man not to touch a woman" (1 Cor 7:1), and "He who has no wife thinks on the things of God, how he can please God. But he who is joined in marriage thinks on the affairs of the world, how he can please his wife" (1 Cor 7:32–33). Had I paid careful attention to these sayings and "become a eunuch for the sake of the kingdom of heaven" (Mt 19:12), I would have been happier finding fulfilment in your embraces.

But I in my misery seethed and followed the driving force of my impulses, abandoning you. I exceeded all the bounds set by your law, and did not escape your chastisement—indeed no mortal can do so. For you were always with me, mercifully punishing me, touching with a bitter taste all my illicit pleasures. Your intention was that I should seek delights unspoilt by disgust and that, in my quest where I could achieve this, I should discover it to be in nothing except you Lord, nothing but you. You "fashion pain to be a lesson" (Ps 93:20), you "strike to heal," you bring death upon us so that we should not die apart from you (Deut 32:39).

Where was I in the sixteenth year of the age of my flesh? "Far away in exile from the pleasures of your house" (Mic 2:9). Sensual folly assumed domination over me, and I gave myself totally to it in acts allowed by shameful humanity but under your laws illicit. My family did not try to extricate me from my headlong course by means of marriage. The only concern was that I should learn to speak as effectively as possible and carry conviction by my oratory.

During my sixteenth year there was an interruption in my studies. I was recalled from Madauros, the nearby town where I had first lived away from home to learn literature and oratory. During that time funds were gathered in preparation for a more distant absence at Carthage, for which my father had more enthusiasm than cash, since he was a citizen of Thagaste with very modest resources. To whom do I tell these things? Not to you, my God. But before you I declare this to my race, to the human race, though only a tiny part can light on this composition of mine. And why do I include this episode? It is that I and any of my readers may reflect on the great depth from which we have to cry to you (Ps 129:1). Nothing is nearer to your ears than a confessing heart and a life grounded in faith (cf. Rom 10:9). At that time everybody was full of praise for my father because he spent money on his son beyond the means of his estate, when that was necessary to finance an education entailing a long journey. Many citizens of far greater wealth did nothing of the kind for their children. But this same father did not care what character before you I was developing, or how chaste I was so long as I possessed a cultured tongue—though my culture really meant a desert uncultivated by you, God. You are the one true and good lord of your land, which is my heart.

In my sixteenth year idleness interposed because of my family's lack
of funds. I was on holiday from all schooling and lived with my parents.
The thorns of lust rose above my head, and there was no hand to root
them out. Indeed, when at the bathhouse my father saw that I was showing signs of virility and the stirrings of adolescence, he was overjoyed to
suppose that he would now be having grandchildren, and told my
mother so. His delight was that of the intoxication which makes the
world oblivious of you, its Creator, and to love your creation instead of
you. He was drunk with the invisible wine of his perverse will directed
downwards to inferior things. But in my mother's heart you had already
begun your temple and the beginning of your holy habitation (Sir
24:14). My father was still a catechumen and had become that only recently. So she shook with a pious trepidation and a holy fear (2 Cor
7:15). For, although I had not yet become a baptized believer, she feared
the twisted paths along which walk those who turn their backs and not
their face towards you (Jer 2:27).

Wretch that I am, do I dare to say that you, my God, were silent when
in reality I was travelling farther from you? Was it in this sense that you
kept silence to me? Then whose words were they but yours which you
were chanting in my ears through my mother, your faithful servant? But
nothing of that went down into my heart to issue in action. Her concern
(and in the secret of my conscience I recall the memory of her admoni-
tion delivered with vehement anxiety) was that I should not fall into fornication, and above all that I should not commit adultery with someone
else's wife. These warnings seemed to me womanish advice which I
would have blushed to take the least notice of. But they were your warnings and I did not realize it. I believed you were silent, and that it was
only she who was speaking, when you were speaking to me through her.
In her you were scorned by me, by me her son, the son of your handmaid, your servant (Ps 115:16). But I did not realize this and went on my
way headlong with such blindness that among my peer group I was
ashamed not to be equally guilty of shameful behaviour when I heard
them boasting of their sexual exploits. Their pride was the more aggres-
sive, the more debauched their acts were; they derived pleasure not
merely from the lust of the act but also from the admiration it evoked.
What is more worthy of censure than vice? Yet I went deeper into vice to
avoid being despised, and when there was no act by admitting to which
I could rival my depraved companions, I used to pretend I had done

things I had not done at all, so that my innocence should not lead my companions to scorn my lack of courage, and lest my chastity be taken as a mark of inferiority.

Such were the companions with whom I made my way through the streets of Babylon. With them I rolled in its dung as if rolling in spices and precious ointments (Song 4:14). To tie me down the more tenaciously to Babylon's belly, the invisible enemy trampled on me (Ps 55:3) and seduced me because I was in the mood to be seduced. The mother of my flesh already had fled from the centre of Babylon (Jer 51:6), but still lingered in the outskirts of the city. Although she had warned me to guard my virginity, she did not seriously pay heed to what her husband had told her about me, and which she felt to hold danger for the future: for she did not seek to restrain my sexual drive within the limit of the marriage bond, if it could not be cut back to the quick. The reason why she showed no such concern was that she was afraid that the hope she placed in me could be impeded by a wife. This was not the hope which my mother placed in you for the life to come, but the hope which my parents entertained for my career that I might do well out of the study of literature. Both of them, as I realized, were very ambitious for me: my father because he hardly gave a thought to you at all, and his ambitions for me were concerned with mere vanities; my mother because she thought it would do no harm and would be a help to set me on the way towards you, if I studied the traditional pattern of a literary education. That at least is my conjecture as I try to recall the characters of my parents.

The reins were relaxed to allow me to amuse myself. There was no strict discipline to keep me in check, which led to an unbridled dissoluteness in many different directions. In all of this there was a thick mist shutting me off from the brightness of your face, my God, and my iniquity as it were "burst out from my fatness" (Ps 72:7).

[...]

"You put forth your hand from on high" (Ps 143:7), and from this deep darkness "you delivered my soul" (Ps 85:13). For my mother, your faithful servant, wept for me before you more than mothers weep when lamenting their dead children. By the "faith and spiritual discernment" (Gal 5:5) which she had from you, she perceived the death which held me, and you heard her, Lord. You heard her and did not despise her tears which poured forth to wet the ground under her eyes in every place where she prayed. You heard her. Hence she was granted the dream by which you encouraged her to allow me to live with her and to have me at the same table in the house. She had begun by refusing me, in her revulsion from and detestation of the blasphemies of my error. Her vision was of herself standing on a rule made of wood. A young man came to her, handsome, cheerful, and smiling to her at a time when she was sad and "crushed with grief" (Lam 1:13). He asked her the reasons why she was downcast and daily in floods of tears—the question being intended, as is usual in such visions, to teach her rather than to learn the answer. She had replied that she mourned my perdition. He then told her to have no anxiety and exhorted her to direct her attention and to see that where she was, there was I also. When she looked, she saw me standing beside her on the same rule. How could this vision come to her unless "your ears were close to her heart" (Ps 10:17)? You are good and all-powerful, caring for each one of us as though the only one in your care, and yet for all as for each individual.

Moreover, what was the source of the fact that when she had recounted the vision to me, I tried to twist its meaning to signify that she should not despair of becoming what I was? But she instantly replied without a moment's hesitation: "The word spoken to me was not 'Where he is, there will you be also,' but 'Where you are, there will he be also.'" I confess to you Lord that to the best of my memory (and it is a matter which I have frequently discussed) I was more moved by your answer through my vigilant mother than by the dream itself. My misinterpretation seemed very plausible. She was not disturbed and quickly saw what was there to be seen, and what I certainly had not seen before she spoke. By the dream the joy of this devout woman, to be fulfilled much later, was predicted many years in advance to give consolation at this time in her anxiety. For almost nine years then followed during which I was "in the deep mire" (Ps 68:3) and darkness of falsehood. Despite my frequent efforts to climb out of it, I was the more heavily plunged back into the filth and wallowed in it. During this time this chaste, devout, and sober widow, one of the kind you love, already cheered by hope but no less constant in prayer and weeping, never ceased her hours of prayer to lament about me to you. Her "prayer entered into your presence" (Ps 87:3). Nevertheless you still let me go on turning over and over again in that darkness.

Meanwhile you gave her another answer that sticks in my memory. For I pass over much because I am hurrying on to those things which especially urge me to make confession to you, and there is much that I do not remember. You gave her another answer through one of your priests, a bishop brought up in the Church and well trained in your books. When that woman asked him to make time to talk to me and refute my errors and correct my evil doctrines and teach me good ones—for he used to do this for those whom perhaps he found suitably disposed—he declined, wisely indeed as I later perceived. For he answered that I was still unready to learn, because I was conceited about the novel excitements of that heresy, and because, as she had informed him, I had already disturbed many untrained minds with many trivial questions. "Let him be where he is," he said; "only pray the Lord for him. By his reading he will discover what an error and how vast an impiety it all is."

At the same time he told her how he himself as a small boy had been handed over to the Manichees by his mother, whom they had led astray. He had not only read nearly all their books but had even copied them. Although he had no one disputing with him and providing a refutation, it had become clear to him that that sect ought to be avoided, and therefore he had left it. When he had said this to her, she was still unwilling to take No for an answer. She pressed him with more begging and with floods of tears, asking him to see me and debate with me. He was now irritated and a little vexed and said: "Go away from me: as you live, it cannot be that the son of these tears should perish." In her conversations with me she often used to recall that she had taken these words as if they had sounded from heaven.

1. What were the ambitions of Augustine's parents for their son?
2. Does Augustine's description of adolescence sound familiar?

Hugh of St. Victor

Various accounts describe Hugh of St. Victor (c. 1090s–1141) as born into a family of the German nobility, or born in Flanders. It is certain that around 1115 he settled at the theologically vibrant monastery of St. Victor in Paris, and there spent the rest of his life teaching and writing. In addition to commenting on various books of the Bible, Hugh contributed significantly to the development of the scholastic mode of organizing theological topics. The following selection exhibits this early scholastic manner of seeking insight into the realities of the Christian life, in this case, of marriage.

BUT MARRIAGE, ACCORDING AS IT IS WORTHY, is a sacrament of that society which exists in spirit between God and the soul. The office of marriage indeed is a sacrament of society, which is in the flesh between Christ and the Church. It is written, he says: "They shall be two in one flesh," (Gen 2:24), and if two are in one flesh, indeed there are not two but one flesh. "This is," as the Apostle says, "the great sacrament in Christ and in the church," (cf. Eph 5:32), to which sacrament woman cannot attain with whom carnal commerce is known not to have taken place. Yet she can attain to another sacrament, not greater in Christ and the Church but greater in God and in the soul. Why? If that which is in the flesh is great, is not this much greater which is in the spirit?

From *On the Sacraments of the Christian Faith*, trans. Roy J. Deferrari (Cambridge, Mass.: Medieval Academy Books, 1951), 326–327, 339–341. Used with kind permission of The Medieval Academy of America.

He says: "It is the spirit that quickeneth: the flesh profiteth nothing," (Jn 6:64). If then that is great which is in the flesh, surely that is much greater which is in the spirit.

If God is rightly called betrothed by Sacred Scripture and the rational spirit is spoken of as betrothed, surely there is something between God and the soul of which whatever exists in marriage between male and female is the sacrament and the image. And perhaps, to speak more specifically, the very association which is preserved externally in marriage by a compact is a sacrament and the substance of the sacrament itself is the mutual love of souls which is guarded in turn by the bond of conjugal society and agreement. And this very love again, by which male and female are united in the sanctity of marriage by their souls, is a sacrament and the sign of that love by which God is joined to the rational soul internally through the infusion of His grace and the participation of His spirit. Therefore, the bond of flesh, which before sin was office in marriage and after sin was granted in the same as a remedy, is thus joined in both ways to marriage so that it is with marriage, is not marriage of itself. For even before it there is true marriage and without it marriage can be holy; then indeed, if that were not present, less fruitfully; but now, if it should not be present, more sincerely. For the fact that after sin the bond of flesh is admitted in marriage is rather a matter of indulgence and compassion, lest the vice of concupiscence, which took root in human flesh after sin, might pour forth disgracefully into every excess, if it could never have been received licitly.

[...]

There are in the main three blessings that accompany marriage, namely, faith, hope of progeny, sacrament. In faith care is taken that there be no lying with another woman or with another man outside the conjugal bond. In hope of progeny care is taken that progeny be expected devoutly, received lovingly, nourished religiously. In the sacrament care is taken that the marriage be not broken and that the man or woman dismissed be not joined with another for the sake of progeny. These are the blessings which marriage places over against that concupiscence of the flesh which still remains in the flesh of sin, without which the mingling of flesh cannot take place. For, as blessed Augustine says, the good of marriage in some manner limits and modifies the evil of the disobeying members, so that carnal concupiscence becomes at least conjugal chastity.

Now this good occurs as a remedy against that evil in two ways, when it restrains that ardor of immoderate lust from unrestrained coition by limiting it under the definite law of one compact, and when it excuses this ardor which would by itself be evil, through the blessings attached to itself. Yet it does not effect that evil not exist at all but that it be not damnable; indeed on account of this good that evil is made venial; for unless it were evil, it would not have need of being excused. And again unless it had a remedy, it would have to be imputed. But if marriage had no good in itself, it could not be a remedy against evil. Now the blessings themselves that are in it excuse the evil which is not sought by it but is tolerated in it, so that that is not imputed to damnation which necessity imposes and the will does not exact. Likewise Augustine says to Valerius: Not only fecundity of which the fruit is in progeny and not only chastity whose bond is faith but also the sacrament of marriage is commended to the married faithful. The essence of this sacrament is that those joined legitimately are not separated as long as they live.

If the faith of marriage is not to know another coition outside marital coition, and the violation of this faith is to commit adultery, it is clear that this blessing so clings to marriage that, if it should indeed be present, as a result of it the marriage would be commended the more, but, if it should not be present, the sacrament of marriage nevertheless would not be annihilated. For as for her who is an adulteress, she is not a wife because she is an adulteress; rather, if she were not a wife, she could not be an adulteress. For there is no adultery except when the faith of the legitimate couch is violated, and surely when this is done, a sin is committed; the sacrament is not made void. Similarly, if hope of progeny is in this, that progeny is awaited devotedly, received lovingly, nourished religiously, there is no doubt that this blessing also cannot always be present in every marriage or in all consorts. For how is progeny hoped for by those who either by a mutual vow maintain continence or from the weakness of age can no longer generate? And so these two, that is, faith and hope of progeny, so accompany marriage that when indeed they are present, in the one case marriage appears more pure, in the other more fruitful, but when they are not present, marriage is proven either more blameworthy or less fruitful, and yet it does not cease to be marriage. But the sacrament seems to be so inseparable that without it marriage cannot exist at all.

So Augustine says: To so great an extent is the nuptial contract the essence of the same sacrament that it is not made void by separation, since while the husband by whom a woman has been left is living, she commits adultery, if she shall marry another. So great a strength of the marriage bond means this, that it would not be so strong unless a certain sacrament of some greater essence were added, which remains unshaken because, though divorce intervene, the nuptial compact is not abolished, so that they are consorts even though separated. For since the two are different, marriage which rests on legitimate association, and the office of marriage which rests on mingling of flesh, in the one indeed, that is marriage, is the sacrament, but to the other, that is to the office of marriage, faith and hope of progeny seem to belong; one, that is faith, so that through it illicit mingling of flesh may be guarded against, the other, that is hope of progeny, that on account of it licit mingling of flesh may be exercised. Just as the office itself of carnal intercourse can be absent from marriage, so too marriage itself can exist without these things which belong to the office of carnal intercourse, although, as it is said, if it should lack faith, it would be less pure, but if it should lack hope of progeny, it would be found less fruitful. For faith has fruit in the chastity of conjugal virtue. Hope of progeny has fruit in the use of fecundity.

Now marriage in marital association itself is a sacrament and on this account, just as the association itself is not divided while both live, so too the sacrament of conjugal association, as long as the marriage exists, is not separated from it. And in this marriage indeed the sacrament externally is undivided association; the essence of the sacrament internally, charity of souls burning mutually and perseveringly. The sacrament externally belongs to Christ and the Church, the essence of the sacrament internally to God and the soul, so that just as in the coition of the flesh we have mentioned the sacrament of Christ and the Church, so also in the compact of the association we show the sacrament of the same. So, this has been said, that it may be shown that sometimes marriage exists without faith and without hope of progeny, but it can never exist without the sacrament, although the sacrament sometimes is found to exist where the sanctity of the sacrament is shown not to exist.

For blessed Augustine says that the sacrament of marriage can be common to all nations, but the sanctity of the sacrament does not exist except in the city of our God and on His holy mount. One can easily see how true this is, if he considers what has been said above. For we said above that in marriage a twofold sacrament existed: one in carnal inter-mingling, the sacrament of that association which exists between Christ and Church; the other in conjugal association, the sacrament of that association which exists between God and soul; or also which was the sacrament of Christ and the Church in the association of marriage; indeed the sacrament of God and the soul in conjugal love. Whether then the sacrament of marriage is accepted in this way or in that, the sacrament of marriage is rightly said to be common to all nations, but the sanctity or virtue of the sacrament does not exist except in the city of our God and on His holy mount, that is, it is said to exist in faith and charity, namely in Holy Church and between the faithful. Now they have the sacrament of marriage who with mutual consent come together to preserve indivisibly and mutually that association which was established by God between male and female. Indeed they alone possess the sanctity of this sacrament, who through faith have been made members of Christ, and through charity have been united to God internally by the mind and devotion.

1. What are the three main blessings that accompany marriage, according to Hugh?
2. Describe the sacramental understanding of marriage.
3. What does Hugh say about divorce?

St. Thomas Aquinas

As a young man St. Thomas Aquinas (1225–1274) joined the new Dominican Order. After studying under the great Dominican theologian St. Albert the Great, Aquinas went on to teach at the University of Paris and elsewhere. A prolific author, he produced commentaries on numerous books of the Scriptures as well as the works of Aristotle. He is best known for his *Summa Theologiae*, which sets forth the mysteries of Christian faith in a balanced and keenly insightful fashion. The following excerpt from Aquinas's *Commentary on the Gospel of St. John*, written in the rather forbidding style of high scholastic biblical commentaries, makes clear the goodness of marriage and its profound theological symbolism.

Chapter 2 of the Gospel of John: Lecture 1

1 On the third day there was a wedding at Cana in Galilee, and the mother of Jesus was there. 2 Jesus and his disciples were also invited to the feast. 3 When the wine ran out, the mother of Jesus said to him, "They have no more wine." 4 Jesus then said to her, "Woman, what does that have to do with me and you? My time has not yet come." 5 His mother said to the servants, "Do whatever he tells you." 6 Now there were six stone water jars near by for purifications according to Jewish customs, each holding two or three metretes. 7

From *Commentary on the Gospel of Saint John*, trans. James A. Weisheipl, O.P. and Fabian Larcher, O.P., part 1 (Albany, N.Y.: Magi Books, 1980), 149–159.

Jesus said to them, "Fill those jars with water." And they filled them to the top.
8 Then Jesus said to them, "Now pour out a drink and take it to the head
waiter." They did as he instructed them. 9 Now when the head waiter tasted
the water made wine, and not knowing where it came from (although the ser-
vants knew, since they had drawn the water), he called the groom over 10 and
said to him, "People usually serve the choice wines first, and when the guests
have had their fill, then they bring out inferior wine; but you have saved the
best wine until now." 11 This beginning of signs Jesus worked in Cana of
Galilee; and Jesus revealed his glory, and his disciples believed in him.

Above, the Evangelist showed the dignity of the incarnate Word and
gave various evidence for it. Now he begins to relate the effects and actions by which the divinity of the incarnate Word was made known to
the world. First, he tells the things Christ did while living in the world,
that show his divinity. Secondly, he tells how Christ showed his divinity
while dying; and this from chapter twelve on.

As to the first he does two things. First, he shows the divinity of Christ
in relation to the power he had over nature. Secondly, in relation to the
effects of grace; and this from chapter three on. Christ's power over nature is pointed out to us by the fact that he changed a nature. And this
change was accomplished by Christ as a sign: first, to his disciples, to
strengthen them; secondly, to the people, to lead them to believe (Jn
2:12). This transformation of a nature, in order to strengthen the disciples, was accomplished at a marriage, when he turned water into wine.
First, the marriage is described. Secondly, those present. Thirdly, the
miracle performed by Christ.

In describing the marriage, the time is first mentioned. Hence he says,
On the third day there was a wedding, i.e., after the calling of the disci-
ples mentioned earlier. For, after being made known by the testimony of
John, Christ also wanted to make himself known. Secondly, the place is
mentioned; hence he says, **at Cana in Galilee**. Galilee is a province, and
Cana a small village located in that province.

As far as the literal meaning is concerned, we should note that there
are two opinions about the time of Christ's preaching. Some say that
there were two and a half years from Christ's baptism until his death. According to them, the events at this wedding took place in the same year
that Christ was baptized. However, both the teaching and practice of the
Church are opposed to this. For three miracles are commemorated on
the feast of the Epiphany: the adoration of the Magi, which took place

in the first year of the Lord's birth; secondly, the baptism of Christ, which implies that he was baptized on the same day thirty years later; thirdly, this marriage, which took place on the same day one year later. It follows from this that at least one year elapsed between his baptism and this marriage. In that year the only things recorded to have been done by the Lord are found in the sixth chapter of Matthew: the fasting in the desert, and the temptation by the devil; and what John tells us in this Gospel of the testimony by the Baptist and the conversion of the disciples. After this wedding, Christ began to preach publicly and to perform miracles up to the time of his passion, so that he preached publicly for two and one half years.

In the mystical sense, marriage signifies the union of Christ with his Church, because as the Apostle says: "This is a great mystery: I am speaking of Christ and his Church" (Eph 5:32). And this marriage was begun in the womb of the Virgin, when God the Father united a human nature to his Son in a unity of person. So, the chamber of this union was the womb of the Virgin: "He established a chamber for the sun" (Ps 18:6). Of this marriage it is said: "The kingdom of heaven is like a king who married his son" (Mt 22:2), that is, when God the Father joined a human nature to his Word in the womb of the Virgin. It was made public when the Church was joined to him by faith: "I will bind you to myself in faith" (Hos 2:20). We read of this marriage: "Blessed are they who are called to the marriage supper of the Lamb" (Rev 19:9). It will be consummated when the bride, i.e., the Church, is led into the resting place of the groom, i.e., into the glory of heaven.

The fact that this marriage took place on the third day is not without its own mystery. For the first day is the time of the law of nature; the second day is the time of the written law; but the third day is the time of grace, when the incarnate Lord celebrated the marriage: "He will revive us after two days; on the third day he will raise us up" (Hos 6:3).

The place too is appropriate. For "Cana" means "zeal," and "Galilee" means "passage." So this marriage was celebrated in the zeal of a passage, to suggest that those persons are most worthy of union with Christ who, burning with the zeal of a conscientious devotion, pass over from the state of guilt to the grace of the Church. "Pass over to me, all who desire me" (Sir 24:26). And they pass from death to life, i.e., from the state of mortality and misery to the state of immortality and glory: "I make all things new" (Rev 21:5).

Then the persons invited are described. Mention is made of three: the mother of Jesus, Jesus himself, and the disciples.

The mother of Jesus is mentioned when he says, **the mother of Jesus was there.** She is mentioned first to indicate that Jesus was still unknown and not invited to the wedding as a famous person, but merely as one acquaintance among others; for as they invited the mother, so also her son. Or, perhaps his mother is invited first because they were uncertain whether Jesus would come to a wedding if invited, because of the unusual piety they noticed in him and because they had not seen him at other social gatherings. So I think that they first asked his mother whether Jesus should be invited. That is why the Evangelist expressly said first that his mother was at the wedding, and that later Jesus was invited.

And this is what comes next: **Jesus was invited.** Christ decided to attend this wedding, first of all, to give us an example of humility. For he did not look to his own dignity, but "just as he condescended to accept the form of a servant, so he did not hesitate to come to the marriage of servants," as Chrysostom says. And as Augustine says: "Let man blush to be proud, for God became humble." For among his other acts of humility, the Son of the Virgin came to a marriage, which he had already instituted in paradise when he was with his Father. Of this example it is said: "Learn from me, for I am gentle and humble of heart" (Mt 11:29).

He came, secondly, to reject the error of those who condemn marriage, for as Bede says: "If there were sin in a holy marriage bed and in a marriage carried out with due purity, the Lord would not have come to the marriage." But because he did come, he implies that the baseness of those who denounce marriage deserves to be condemned. "If she marries, it is not a sin" (1 Cor 7:36).

The disciples are mentioned when he says, **and his disciples.**

In its mystical meaning, the mother of Jesus, the Blessed Virgin, is present in spiritual marriages as the one who arranges the marriage, because it is through her intercession that one is joined to Christ through grace: "In me is every hope of life and of strength" (Sir 24:25). Christ is present as the true groom of the soul, as is said below (Jn 3:29): "It is the groom who has the bride." The disciples are the groomsmen uniting the Church to Christ, the one of whom it is said: "I betrothed you to one husband, to present you as a chaste virgin to Christ" (2 Cor 11:2).

At this physical marriage some role in the miracle belongs to the mother of Christ, some to Christ, and some to the disciples. When he says, **When the wine ran out,** he indicates the part of each. The role of Christ's mother was to superintend the miracle; the role of Christ to perform it; and the disciples were to bear witness to it. As to the first, Christ's mother assumed the role of a mediatrix. Hence she does two things. First, she intercedes with her Son. In the second place, she instructs the servants. As to the first, two things are mentioned. First, his mother's intercession; secondly, the answer of her Son.

In Mary's intercession, note first her kindness and mercy. For it is a quality of mercy to regard another's distress as one's own, because to be merciful is to have a heart distressed at the distress of another: "Who is weak, and I am not weak?" (2 Cor 11:29). And so because the Blessed Virgin was full of mercy, she desired to relieve the distress of others. So he says, **When the wine ran out, the mother of Jesus said to him.**

Note, secondly, her reverence for Christ: for because of the reverence we have for God it is sufficient for us merely to express our needs: "Lord, all my desires are known by you" (Ps 37:10). But it is not our business to wonder about the way in which God will help us, for as it is said: "We do not know what we should pray for as we ought" (Rom 8:26). And so his mother merely told him of their need, saying, **They have no more wine.**

Thirdly, note the Virgin's concern and care. For she did not wait until they were in extreme need, but **When the wine ran out,** that is, immediately. This is similar to what is said of God: "A helper in times of trouble" (Ps 9:10).

Chrysostom asks: Why did Mary never encourage Christ to perform any miracles before this time? For she had been told of his power by the angel, whose work had been confirmed by the many things she had seen happening in his regard, all of which she remembered, thinking them over in her heart (Lk 2:51). The reason is that before this time he lived like any other person. So, because the time was not appropriate, she put off asking him. But now, after John's witness to him and after the conversion of his disciples, she trustingly prompted Christ to perform miracles. In this she was true to the symbol of the synagogue, which is the mother of Christ: for it was customary for the Jews to require miracles: "The Jews require signs" (1 Cor 1:22).

She says to him, **They have no more wine.** Here we should note that before the incarnation of Christ three wines were running out: the wine of justice, of wisdom, and of charity or grace. Wine stings, and in this respect it is a symbol of justice. The Samaritan poured wine and oil into the wounds of the injured man, that is, he mingled the severity of justice with the sweetness of mercy. "You have made us drink the wine of sorrow" (Ps 59:5). But wine also delights the heart, "Wine cheers the heart of man" (Ps 103:15). And in this respect wine is a symbol of wisdom, the meditation of which is enjoyable in the highest degree: "Her companionship has no bitterness" (Wis 8:16). Further, wine intoxicates: "Drink, friends, and be intoxicated, my dearly beloved" (Song 5:1). And in this respect wine is a symbol of charity: "I have drunk my wine with my milk" (Song 5:1). It is also a symbol of charity because of charity's fervor: "Wine makes the virgins flourish" (Zech 9:17).

The wine of justice was indeed running out in the old law, in which justice was imperfect. But Christ brought it to perfection: "Unless your justice is greater than that of the scribes and of the Pharisees, you will not enter into the kingdom of heaven" (Mt 5:20). The wine of wisdom was also running out, for it was hidden and symbolic, because as it says in 1 Corinthians (10:11): "All these things happened to them in symbol." But Christ plainly brought wisdom to light: "He was teaching them as one having authority" (Mt 7:29). The wine of charity was also running out, because they had received a spirit of serving only in fear. But Christ converted the water of fear into the wine of charity when he gave "the spirit of adoption as sons, by which we cry: 'Abba, Father'" (Rom 8:15), and when "the charity of God was poured out into our hearts," as Romans (5:5) says.

Then when he says, **Jesus said to her,** the answer of Christ is given. This answer has been the occasion for three heresies.

The Manicheans claim that Christ had only an imaginary body, not a real one. Valentinus maintained that Christ assumed a celestial body and that, as far as his body was concerned, Christ was not related to the Virgin at all. The source of this error was that he understood, **Woman, what does that have to do with me and you?** as if it meant: "I have received nothing from you." But this is contrary to the authority of Sacred Scripture. For the Apostle says: "God sent his Son, made from a woman" (Gal 4:4). Now Christ could not be said to have been made from her, unless he had taken something from her. Further, Augustine argues against them: "How do you know that our Lord said, **What does that have to do with me and you?** You reply that it is because John says so. But he also says that the Virgin was the mother of Christ. So, if you believe the Evangelist when he states that Jesus said this to his mother, you should also believe him when he says, **and the mother of Jesus was there.**"

Then there was Ebion who said that Christ was conceived from a man's seed, and Elvidius, who said that the Virgin did not remain a virgin after childbirth. They were deceived by the fact that he said, **Woman,** which seems to imply the loss of virginity. But this is false, for in Sacred Scripture the word "woman" sometimes refers merely to the female sex, as it does in "made from a woman" (Gal 4:4). This is obvious also by the fact that Adam, speaking to God about Eve, said: "The woman whom you gave me as a companion, gave me fruit from the tree, and I ate it" (Gen 3:12); for Eve was still a virgin in Paradise, where Adam had not known her. Hence the fact that the mother of Christ is here called "woman" in this Gospel does not imply a loss of virginity, but refers to her sex.

The Priscillianists, however, erred by misunderstanding the words of Christ, **My time has not yet come.** They claimed that all things happen by fate, and that the actions of men, including those of Christ, are subject to predetermined times. And that is why, according to them, Christ said, **My time has not yet come.**

But this is false for any man. For since man has free choice, and this is because he has reason and will, both of which are spiritual, then obviously, as far as choice is concerned, man, so far from being subject to bodies, is really their master. For spiritual things are superior to material things, so much so that the Philosopher says that the wise man is master of the stars. Further, their heresy is even less true of Christ, who is the Lord and Creator of the stars. Thus when he says, **My time has not yet come,** he is referring to the time of his passion, which was fixed for him, not by necessity, according to divine providence. What is said in Sirach (33:7) is also contrary to their opinion: "Why is one day better than another?" And the answer is: "They have been differentiated by the knowledge of the Lord," i.e., they were differentiated from one another not by chance, but by God's providence.

Since we have eliminated the above opinions, let us look for the reason why our Lord answered, **Woman, what does that have to do with me and you?** For Augustine, Christ has two natures, the divine and the human. And although the same Christ exists in each, nevertheless things appropriate to him according to his human nature are distinct from what is appropriate to him according to his divine nature. Now to perform miracles is appropriate to him according to his divine nature, which he received from the Father; while to suffer is according to his human nature, which he received from his mother. So when his mother requests this miracle, he answers, **Woman, what does that have to do with me and you?** as if saying: I did not receive from you that in me which enables me to perform miracles, but that which enables me to suffer, i.e., that which makes it appropriate for me to suffer, i.e., I have received a human nature from you. And so I will recognize you when this weakness hangs on the cross. And so he continues with, **My time has not yet come.** As if to say: I will recognize you as my mother when the time of my passion arrives. And so it was that on the cross he entrusted his mother to the disciple.

Chrysostom explains this differently. He says that the Blessed Virgin, burning with zeal for the honor of her Son, wanted Christ to perform miracles at once, before it was opportune; but that Christ, being much wiser than his mother, restrained her. For he was unwilling to perform the miracle before the need for it was known; otherwise, it would have been less appreciated and less credible. And so he says, **Woman, what does that have to do with me and you?** As if to say: Why bother me? **My time has not yet come,** i.e., I am not yet known to those present. Nor do they know that the wine ran out; and they must first know this, because when they know their need they will have a greater appreciation of the benefit they will receive.

Now although his mother was refused, she did not lose hope in her Son's mercy. So she instructs the servants, **Do whatever he tells you,** in which, indeed, consists the perfection of all justice. For perfect justice consists in obeying Christ in all things: "We will do all that the Lord commanded us" (Ex 29:35). **Do whatever he tells you,** is fittingly said of God alone, for man can err now and then. Hence in matters that are against God, we are not held to obey men: "We ought to obey God rather than men" (Acts 5:29). We ought to obey God, who does not err and cannot be deceived, in all things.

1. Describe the relationship of Christ and his mother, according to Aquinas's interpretation.
2. Why did Christ perform his first miracle at a marriage?

St. Birgitta of Sweden

St. Birgitta of Sweden (1302–1373) was born in Sweden and died in Rome. One of her eight children, Catherine, is venerated as a saint. After the death of her husband of almost thirty years, she established a religious community for women, the Bridgettines, in 1346. In 1349 she went to Rome, where she lived for the rest of her life. With St. Catherine of Siena, she was instrumental in persuading the pope, then residing in Avignon, to return to Rome. The following selection from her Life, written in the hagiographical style of the day, describes her and her husband's efforts to devote themselves to God and to the service of others.

IN THE MEANTIME, LADY BIRGITTA WAS BETROTHED to a rich young man, a noble and prudent knight who was called Lord Ulf of Ulvåsa, prince of Närke. Between them they had so very honorable a marriage that both spouses lived in virginity for one year, devoutly asking God that if they ought to come together he, the Creator of all, would from them create an offspring that would be at his service. She truly loved God and was most highly wary of herself so that no one might speak badly of her and that she might not give occasion for anyone to disparage her. Therefore she fled levities and places or persons for which she

Excerpts from *Birgitta of Sweden: Life and Selected Revelations*, ed. Marguerite Tjader Harris, trans. Albert Ryle Kezel, The Classics of Western Spirituality Series (Mahwah, N.J.: Paulist Press, 1990), 74–77. Copyright © 1990 by the Order of St. Birgitta, Rome. Translation, notes, and foreword copyright © 1990 by Albert Ryle Kezel, New York/Mahwah, N.J. Used with permission of Paulist Press. www.paulistpress.com

could be branded; and she had in her company honest handmaids and well-mannered companions. Indeed, together with the members of her household, she was intent upon work for divine worship or for the welfare of her neighbors.

In truth, the bride of Christ was so very fervent in prayer and tears that when her husband was away, she passed almost whole nights in vigil and did not spare her body many genuflexions and cruel disciplining. In fact, some time passed during which she constantly kept asking God in her prayers that some suitable manner of praying might be poured into her. One day, in a wonderful manner, she was elevated in mind; and then there was poured into her a most beautiful prayer concerning the passion of Christ and concerning the life and the praise of the most Blessed Virgin Mary. She kept this prayer in her memory so that afterward she might read it every day. And so one time when blessed Mary appeared to her afterward, she said: "I merited that prayer for you; therefore when you read it, you will be visited with the consolation of my Son."

She continuously frequented confession; and for her confessor, she had a very expert and devout master of theology, called Master Matthias, who wrote an excellent gloss on the whole Bible and composed many volumes of books. And it was he who composed the prologue for the books of the *Heavenly Revelations* of the aforesaid Lady Birgitta; and it was him that she obeyed in all her difficulties. Wherefore, this same confessor used to say familiarly to his friends: "In Lady Birgitta, it is a sign of some future grace that she so laments light matters as others lament things very serious and that she leaves nothing in her words or behavior unexamined."

When she could, she multiplied her great fasts and other acts of abstinence; and she very often abstained from delicacies in a hidden way so that it would not be noticed by her husband or by others.

Indeed, when she was not occupied with manual labor, she was continually rereading the lives of the saints and the Bible, which she had caused to be written out for herself in her own language; and when she could hear the sermons of upright men, she did not spare herself the labor of going to hear those same sermons.

Right up to her death, she did very large almsdeeds. In Sweden, she had a house set aside for the poor; and she served them in person when she could. She washed their feet and clothed them and visited them when they were infirm and handled their wounds and bodies with tender compassion and the greatest of maternal charity.

Now at one time Lady Birgitta was imperiled during childbirth, and her life was despaired of. That night, the women who were present to watch over her were awake; and as they looked, a person dressed in white silk was seen to enter and stand before the bed and handle each one of Lady Birgitta's members as she lay there—to the fear of all the women who were present. When, however, that person had gone out, Lady Birgitta gave birth so easily that it was a thing of wonder and not to be doubted that the Blessed Virgin, who gave birth without pain, was that person who mitigated the labors, the pains, and the peril of her handmaid, just as that same Virgin afterwards told her in a vision when she spoke this revelation:

"When you," she said, "had difficulty in childbirth, I, Mary, entered unto you. For that reason, you are an ingrate if you do not love me. Labor, therefore, that your children may also be my children."

The bride of Christ, therefore, with great concern and diligence, virtuously educated and nurtured her sons and daughters, handing them over to teachers by whom they were instructed in discipline and good behavior. She wept daily over her children's sins, fearing that they would offend their God. And so one time when Saint John the Baptist appeared to her, he said: "Because you wept over the fact that your son offended me by not fasting on my vigil, and because you would prefer him to serve me rather than be a king, I shall therefore help him and shall arm him with my arms." Mention is made of this more clearly at the end of the fourth book of the *Heavenly Revelations* given to the aforesaid lady.

When, however, Lady Birgitta had for a long time been making progress in the virtues, she also gained her husband for God. For even though he was a vigorous man and an important member of the king of Sweden's council, he occupied himself—at his wife's advice and admonishment—in learning to read the Hours of the most Blessed Virgin Mary and the books containing the laws and legal judgments; and he studied to fulfill what belongs to justice and the law. And so, both of them—namely, this husband and wife—being fervent in their love for God and that they might more freely disengage themselves from the vanities of the world, went forth from their fatherland and from their kindred after Abraham's example, and, with great labors and expenses, proceeded into Spain to Saint James in Compostella. After they had made their pilgrimage to many places of the saints and while they were on the way back, her husband took sick in the city that is called Arras, near Flanders. As the sickness grew worse, the bride of

Christ, being in a state of great anxiety of soul, merited to be consoled by Saint Denis, who appeared and spoke to her at prayer: "I," he said, "am Denis, who came from Rome to these parts of France to proclaim God's word in my life. And so, because you love me with special devotion, I therefore proclaim to you that through you, God wills to be made known to the world and that you have been handed over to my guardianship and protection. Wherefore I shall help you always; and I give to you this sign: your husband will not die now of this sickness." And many other times, this same blessed Denis visited her in revelations and consoled her.

After some days, there in that same city of Arras, she again saw certain wonderful things in prophetic vision: namely, how she was going to travel to Rome and to the holy city of Jerusalem, and how she was going to depart from this world, and how a very handsome youth led her then in spirit through all the said places. All these things were thus fulfilled after much time.

However, after his long illness, her husband was convalescing; and they both returned to their fatherland. Between them, they maintained a mutual continence and decided to enter a monastery. And after all their affairs and goods had been set in order to this end, her husband—still having the same purpose—died in the year of our Lord, 1344.

1. What would it be like to live with so much attention to eternal life?
2. Describe Birgitta's concern for the welfare of her husband and children.

St. Thomas More

St. Thomas More (1478–1535), who served as Chancellor of England, was beheaded in 1535 for refusing to acknowledge King Henry VIII's supremacy over the Church in England. In addition to practicing law and to his political career, he wrote numerous works, the most famous of which is *Utopia*, as a leading figure in the English Renaissance. A friend of Erasmus, More was also an important theological writer. In the letter below, to the tutor of his daughter, he displays the virtues of a good father.

At Court, 22 May [1518?]

I HAVE RECEIVED, MY DEAR GONELL, YOUR LETTER, elegant and full of affection as always. Your devotion to my children I perceive from your letter, your diligence from theirs. Everyone's letter pleased me greatly, but above all that I notice Elizabeth shows a modesty of character in the absence of her mother, which not every girl would show in her mother's presence. Let her understand that such conduct delights me more than all the learning in the world. Though I prefer learning joined with virtue to all the treasures of kings, yet renown for learning, if you take away moral probity, brings nothing else but notorious and noteworthy infamy, especially in a woman. Since erudition in women is a new thing and a reproach to the sloth of men, many will gladly assail it, and impute

From "Letter to William Gonell," in *St. Thomas More: Selected Letters*, ed. Elizabeth Frances Rogers (New Haven, Conn.: Yale University Press, 1961), 103–107. Used with kind permission of Yale University Press.

to learning what is really the fault of nature, thinking from the vices of the learned to get their own ignorance esteemed as virtue. On the other hand, if a woman (and this I desire and hope with you as their teacher for all my daughters) to eminent virtue of mind should add even moderate skill in learning, I think she will gain more real good than if she obtain the riches of Croesus and the beauty of Helen. Not because that learning will be a glory to her, though learning will accompany virtue as a shadow does a body, but because the reward of wisdom is too solid to be lost with riches or to perish with beauty, since it depends on the inner knowledge of what is right, not on the talk of men, than which nothing is more foolish or mischievous.

For as it becomes a good man to avoid infamy, so to lay oneself out for renown is the sign of a man who is not only arrogant, but ridiculous and miserable. A mind must be uneasy which ever wavers between joy and sadness because of other men's opinions. Among all the benefits that learning bestows on men, I think there is none more excellent than that by study we are taught to seek in that very study not praise, but utility. Such has been the teaching of the most learned men, especially of philosophers, who are the guides of human life, although some may have abused learning, like other good things, simply to court empty glory and popular renown.

I have written at length on not pursuing glory, my dear Gonell, because of what you say in your letter, that Margaret's lofty and exalted character of mind should not be debased. In this judgment I quite agree with you; but to me, and, no doubt, to you also, that man would seem to debase a generous character of mind who would accustom it to admire what is vain and low. He, on the contrary, raises it who rises to virtue and true goods, and who looks down with contempt from the contemplation of the sublime, on those shadows of good things which almost all mortals, through ignorance of truth, greedily snatch at as if they were true goods.

Therefore, my dearest Gonell, since I thought we must walk by this road, I have often begged not you only, who, out of your exceptional affection for all my family, would do it of your own accord, nor only my wife, who is sufficiently urged by her truly maternal love for them, which has been proved to me in many ways, but absolutely all my friends, continually to warn my children to avoid as it were the precipices of pride and haughtiness, and to walk in the pleasant meadows of modesty: not to be dazzled at the sight of gold; not to lament the lack of what they erroneously admire in others; not to think more of themselves for gaudy trappings, nor less for the want of them; not to deform the beauty that nature has given them by neglect, nor to try to heighten it by artifice; to put virtue in the first place among goods, learning in the second; and in their studies to esteem most whatever may teach them piety towards God, charity to all, and modesty and Christian humility in themselves. By such means they will receive from God the reward of an innocent life, and in the assured expectation of it will view death without dread, and meanwhile possessing solid joy will neither be puffed up by the empty praise of men, nor dejected by evil tongues. These I consider the real and genuine fruits of learning, and though I admit that all literary men do not possess them, I would maintain that those who give themselves to study with such intent will easily attain their end and become perfect.

Nor do I think that the harvest is much affected whether it is a man or a woman who does the sowing. They both have the name of human being whose nature reason differentiates from that of beasts; both, I say, are equally suited for the knowledge of learning by which reason is cultivated, and, like plowed land, germinates a crop when the seeds of good precepts have been sown. But if the soil of a woman be naturally bad, and apter to bear fern than grain, by which saying many keep women from study, I think, on the contrary, that a woman's wit is the more diligently to be cultivated, so that nature's defect may be redressed by industry. This was the opinion of the ancients, both the wisest and the most saintly. Not to speak of the rest, Jerome and Augustine not only exhorted excellent matrons and honorable virgins to study, but also, in order to assist them, diligently explained the abstruse meanings of the Scriptures, and wrote for tender girls letters replete with so much erudition that nowadays old men who call themselves doctors of sacred literature can scarcely read them correctly, much less understand them. Do you, my learned Gonell, have the kindness to see that my daughters thoroughly learn these works of saintly men. From them they will learn in particular what goal they should set for their studies, and the whole fruit of their endeavors should consist in the testimony of God and a good conscience. Thus they will be inwardly calm and at peace and neither stirred by praise of flatterers nor stung by the follies of unlearned mockers of learning.

But I fancy that I now hear you object that these precepts, though true, are beyond the tender years of my daughters, since you will scarcely find a man, however old and advanced in study, whose mind is so fixed and firm as not to be tickled sometimes with desire of glory. But, dear Gonell, the more do I see the difficulty of getting rid of this pest of pride, the more do I see the necessity of getting to work at it from childhood. For I find no other reason why this inescapable evil so clings to our hearts, than that almost as soon as we are born, it is sown in the tender minds of children by their nurses, it is cultivated by their teachers, it is nourished and brought to maturity by their parents; while no one teaches anything, even the good, without bidding them always to expect praise as the recompense and prize of virtue. Thus long accustomed to magnify praise, they strive to please the greater number (that is, the worse) and end by being ashamed to be good. That this plague of vainglory may be banished far from my children, may you, my dear Gonell, and their mother and all their friends, sing this song to them, and repeat it, and beat it into their heads, that vainglory is despicable, and to be spit upon, and that there is nothing more sublime than that humble modesty so often praised by Christ; and this your prudent charity will so enforce as to teach virtue rather than reprove vice, and make them love good advice instead of hating it. To this purpose nothing will more conduce than to read to them the lessons of the ancient Fathers, who, they know, cannot be angry with them; and, as they honor them for their sanctity, they must needs be much moved by their authority. If you will read something of this sort, besides their reading of Sallust—to Margaret and Elizabeth, who are more mature than John and Cecily—you will bind me and them, already in your debt, still more to you. And besides you will make my children who are dear to me first by the law of nature, and then dearer by learning and virtue, most dear by such advancement in knowledge and good character. Farewell.

From the Court, on the vigil of Pentecost.

1. Why does Thomas More insist upon the education of his daughter?
2. How, according to More, should parents respond to the danger of pride?

St. Teresa of Avila

St. Teresa of Avila (1515–1582) entered the Carmelite Monastery of the Incarnation at Avila at the age of twenty. Known for her reform of the
Carmelite movement, assisted by St. John of the Cross, she wrote a number of spiritual masterpieces, including *The Interior Castle, The Way of Perfection*, and her *Autobiography*. The following brief selection from her autobiography describes her experience of family life. I have chosen this
selection because of its testimony both to the impact that parents can have
upon their children and to the difficult nature of adolescence.

TO HAVE HAD VIRTUOUS AND GOD-FEARING PARENTS along with the
graces the Lord granted me should have been enough for me to have
led a good life, if I had not been so wretched. My father was fond of
reading good books, and thus he also had books in Spanish for his children to read. These good books together with the care my mother took
to have us pray and be devoted to our Lady and to some of the saints
began to awaken me when, I think, six or seven years old, to the practice
of virtue. It was a help to me to see that my parents favored nothing but
virtue. And they themselves possessed many.

From *The Collected Works of St. Teresa of Avila*, vol. 1, *The Book of Her Life*, trans. Kieran Ka-
vanaugh, O.C.D., and Otilio Rodriguez, O.C.D. (Washington, D.C.: ICS Publications, 1976),
33–38. Used with kind permission of ICS Publications, Institute of Carmelite Studies. Copyright © 1976 by Washington Province of Discalced Carmelites. ICS Publications, 2131 Lincoln
Rd, NE, Washington, D.C. 20002-1199, U.S.A. www.icspublications.org

My father was a man very charitable with the poor and compassionate toward the sick, and even toward servants. So great was his compassion that nobody was ever able to convince him to accept slaves. And his pity for them was such that once having in his home a slave owned by his brother, he treated her as though she were one of his children. He used to say that out of pity he couldn't bear seeing her held captive. He was very honest. No one ever saw him swear or engage in fault-finding. He was an upright man.

My mother also had many virtues. And she suffered much sickness during her life. She was extremely modest. Although very beautiful, she never gave occasion to anyone to think she paid any attention to her beauty. For at the time of her death at the age of thirty-three, her clothes were already those of a much older person. She was gentle and very intelligent. Great were the trials she suffered during her life. Her death was a truly Christian one.

We were in all three sisters and nine brothers. All resembled their parents in being virtuous, through the goodness of God, with the exception of myself—although I was the most loved of my father. And it seemed he was right—before I began to offend God. For I am ashamed when I recall the good inclinations the Lord gave me and how poorly I knew how to profit by them.

My brothers and sisters did not in any way hold me back from the service of God. I had one brother about my age. We used to get together to read the lives of the saints. (He was the one I liked most, although I had great love for them all and they for me.) When I considered the martyrdoms the saints suffered for God, it seemed to me that the price they paid for going to enjoy God was very cheap, and I greatly desired to die in the same way. I did not want this on account of the love I felt for God but to get to enjoy very quickly the wonderful things I read there were in heaven. And my brother and I discussed together the means we should take to achieve this. We agreed to go off to the land of the Moors and beg them, out of love of God, to cut off our heads there. It seemed to me the Lord had given us courage at so tender an age, but we couldn't discover any means. Having parents seemed to us the greatest obstacle. We were terrified in what we read about the suffering and the glory that was to last forever. We spent a lot of time talking about this and took delight in often repeating: forever and ever and ever. As I said this over and over, the Lord was pleased to impress upon me in childhood the way of truth.

When I saw it was impossible to go where I would be killed for God, we made plans to be hermits. And in a garden that we had in our house, we tried as we could to make hermitages piling up some little stones which afterwards would quickly fall down again. And so in nothing could we find a remedy for our desire. It gives me devotion now to see how God gave me so early what I lost through my own fault.

I gave what alms I could, but that was little. I sought out solitude to pray my devotions, and they were many, especially the rosary, to which my mother was very devoted; and she made us devoted to it too. When I played with other girls I enjoyed it when we pretended we were nuns in a monastery, and it seemed to me that I desired to be one, although not as much as I desired the other things I mentioned.

I remember that when my mother died I was twelve years old or a little less. When I began to understand what I had lost, I went, afflicted, before an image of our Lady and besought her with many tears to be my mother. It seems to me that although I did this in simplicity it helped me. For I have found favor with this sovereign Virgin in everything I have asked of her, and in the end she has drawn me to herself. It wearies me now to see and think that I was not constant in the good desires I had in my childhood.

O my Lord, since it seems You have determined to save me, I beseech Your Majesty that it may be so. And since You have granted me as many favors as You have, don't You think it would be good (not for my gain but for Your honor) if the inn where You have so continually to dwell were not to get so dirty? It wearies me, Lord, even to say this, for I know that the whole fault was mine. It doesn't seem to me that there was anything more for You to do in order that from this age I would be all Yours. If I start to complain about my parents, I am not able to do so, for I saw nothing but good in them and solicitude for my own good.

As I grew older, when I began to know of the natural attractive qualities the Lord had bestowed on me (which others said were many), instead of thanking Him for them, I began to make use of them all to offend Him, as I shall now tell.

What I am going to tell about began, it seems to me, to do me much harm. I sometimes reflect on the great damage parents do by not striving that their children might always see virtuous deeds of every kind. For even though my mother, as I said, was so virtuous, I did not, in reaching the age of reason, imitate her good qualities; in fact hardly at all. And the bad ones did me much harm. She loved books of chivalry. But this pastime didn't hurt her the way it did me, for she did not fail to do her duties; and we used to read them together in our free time. Perhaps she did this reading to escape thinking of the great trials she had to bear and to busy her children with something so that they would not turn to other things dangerous to them. Our reading such books was a matter that weighed so much upon my father that we had to be cautioned lest he see us. I began to get the habit of reading these books. And by that little fault, which I saw in my mother, I started to grow cold in my desires and to fail in everything else. I didn't think it was wrong to waste many hours of the day and night in such a useless practice, even though hidden from my father. I was so completely taken up with this reading that I didn't think I could be happy if I didn't have a new book.

I began to dress in finery and to desire to please and look pretty, taking great care of my hands and hair and about perfumes and all the empty things in which one can indulge, and which were many, for I was very vain. I had no bad intentions since I would not have wanted anyone to offend God on my account. For many years I took excessive pains about cleanliness and other things that did not seem in any way sinful. Now I see how wrong it must have been.

I had some first cousins who often came to our house, though my father was very cautious and would not allow others to do so; please God he had been inspired to do likewise with my cousins. For now I realize what a danger it is at an age when one should begin to cultivate the virtues to associate with people who do not know the vanity of the world but rather are just getting ready to throw themselves into it. They were about my age—a little older than I—and we always went about together. They liked me very much, and I engaged in conversations with them about all the things that pleased them. I listened to accounts of their affections and of childish things not the least bit edifying; and, what was worse, I exposed my soul to that which caused all its harm.

If I should have to give advice, I would tell parents that when their children are this age they ought to be very careful about whom their children associate with. For here lies the root of great evil since our natural bent is toward the worst rather than toward the best.

So it happened to me. For I had a sister much older than I whose modesty and goodness (of which she had a great deal) I did not imitate at all; and I imitated all that was harmful in a relative who spent a lot of time at our house. She was so frivolous that my mother tried very hard to keep her from coming to our home. It seems my mother foresaw the harm that would be done to me on account of her, but there were so many occasions for her to come to the house that my mother could not prevent it. This relative was the one I liked to associate with. My talks and conversations were with her, for she encouraged me in all the pastimes I desired and even immersed me in them by sharing with me her conversations and vanities. Until I began to associate with her when I was fourteen, or I think older (I mean when she took me for her friend and confidante), I don't think I would have abandoned God by a mortal sin or lost the fear of God, although the fear of losing my honor was stronger in me. This sense of honor gave me the strength not to completely lose my reputation. Nor do I think anything in the world could have made me change my mind in that regard. Neither do I think the love of anyone could have made me give in. Would that I had had the fortitude not to do anything against the honor of God just as my natural bent gave me fortitude not to lose anything of what I thought belonged to the honor of the world. And I did not see that I was losing it in many other ways.

I was extreme in my vain desire for my reputation, but the means necessary to preserve it I didn't take; although I was very circumspect so as not to lose it entirely.

This friendship pained my father and sister. They often reproached me for it. Since they couldn't do away with the occasion for her coming to our home, their careful efforts were useless, for I was strikingly shrewd when it came to mischief. It frightens me sometimes to think of the harm a bad companion can do, and if I hadn't experienced it I wouldn't believe it. Especially during adolescence the harm done must be greater. I should like parents to learn from my experience to be very watchful in this matter. And indeed this conversation so changed me that hardly any virtue remained to my naturally virtuous soul. And I think she and another girlfriend of the same type impressed their own traits upon me.

From such experience I understand the great profit that comes from good companionship. And I am certain that if at that age I had gone around with virtuous persons, I would have remained whole in virtue. For should I have had, when that age, someone to teach me to fear God, my soul would have gained strength not to fall. Afterward, having lost this fear of God completely, I only had the fear of losing my reputation, and such fear brought me torment in everything I did. With the thought that my deeds would not be known, I dared to do many things truly against my honor and against God.

These things did me harm, I think, at the beginning, and it wasn't her fault but mine. For afterward my malice was sufficient, together with having the maids around, for in them I found a helping hand for every kind of wrong. If there had been one of them to give me good counsel, I perhaps would have benefited by it; but self-interest blinded them as my vanity did me. I was never inclined to great evil—for I naturally abhorred indecent things—but to the pastime of pleasant conversation; yet, placed in the occasion, the danger was at hand, and my father's and brothers' reputation was in jeopardy as well. From all these occasions and dangers God delivered me in such a way that it seems clear He strove, against my will, to keep me from being completely lost, although this deliverance could not be achieved so secretly as to prevent me from suffering much loss of reputation and my father from being without suspicion. For it doesn't seem to me that three months during which I engaged in these vanities had gone by when my father brought me to a convent in that place where they educated persons like myself, although not with habits as bad as mine. This was done so cautiously that only I and some relatives knew about it because they waited for an opportunity when it would not seem surprising for me to go to the convent school; that is, once my sister was married it seemed no longer good for me to stay at home without a mother.

So excessive was the love my father bore me and so great my dissimulation that he was unable to believe there was much wrong with me, and so he was not angered with me. Since this period of time had been brief, and though he knew something, nothing could be said with certainty. For since I feared so much for my honor, I used every effort to keep my actions secret, and I never considered that one can never do this with Him who sees all things. O my God! What harm is done in the world by considering our actions of only little importance and by thinking something can be done against You in secret! I am certain that great evils would be avoided if we were to understand that the whole matter lies not in our guarding ourselves against men but in our guarding ourselves against displeasing You.

1. Describe Teresa's family, including her extended family.
2. Why is adolescence a difficult time?

St. Jane de Chantal

St. Jane de Chantal (1572–1641), the daughter of a lawyer, married at age twenty Baron Christophe de Rabutin-Chantal. Her marriage was a happy one, but cut short by a tragic hunting accident that killed her husband shortly after the birth of their last child. The couple had six children, four of whom survived infancy. In 1604, she met St. Francis de Sales, the young bishop of Geneva, and in 1610 they cofounded a religious community for women, the Visitation of Holy Mary. Marked by a concern to practice in daily life a complete trust in the workings of divine Providence, their practical spirituality was aimed at Christians living in the world. This practical spirituality is on display in her letters over the years to her daughter Françon.

Live + Jesus !   [Paris, 1620]

DARLING, SINCE M. DE TOULONJON IS FREE for eight or ten days, he is hurrying off to see you to find out firsthand whether you think he is suitable for you or not. He hopes his personality will not displease you. As for me, frankly, I see nothing to find fault with in him; in fact, I couldn't wish for more. Our Lord has given me so much satisfaction about this match that I can't remember ever having had such a good

Excerpts from "Letters to Françoise de Chantal (Madame de Toulonjon)," trans. Péronne Marie Thibert, V.H.M., in *Francis de Sales, Jane de Chantal: Letters of Spiritual Direction*, Classics of Western Spirituality Series (Mahwah, N.J.: Paulist Press, 1988), 210–219. Copyright © 1988 by Péronne Marie Thibert, V.H.M., Wendy M. Wright, and Joseph F. Power, O.S.F.S. Used with permission of Paulist Press. www.paulistpress.com

feeling about a temporal matter. I am not so much attracted by his good
background and refinement, as by his intelligence, pleasant disposition,
sincerity, sound judgment, integrity, and good reputation. In a word,
dear Françon, let us thank God for such a match.

Out of gratitude, dear, try to love and serve God better than you ever
have, and don't let anything stop you from continuing to go frequently
to the sacraments or from trying to be humble and gentle. Take the *Devout Life* for your guide; it will lead you safely. Don't waste time fussing
about jewelry and fashions. You will be living in plenty, but, my darling,
remember always that we are meant to use the good things God gives us
without being attached to them. Such is the attitude we should have toward all that the world values. From now on, try to live honorably, modestly, sensibly, in the new way of life that is before you.

I'm certainly very happy that your relatives and I arranged this marriage without you, for this is how things should be, and, dearest, I want
you always to follow my advice. Moreover, your brother, who has good
judgment, is delighted about your engagement. True, M. de Toulonjon is
about fifteen years older than you, but, darling, you will be much happier
with him than with some rash, dissolute, young fool like the young men
of today. You are marrying a man who is not at all like this; he is not a
gambler, has lived honorably at court and on the battlefield, has received
high appointments from the king. You would be lacking the good sense I
believe you to have if you didn't accept him cordially and sincerely. I beg
you, dear, accept him graciously, and be assured that God who has been
mindful of you will not forget you if you abandon yourself to His tender
care, for He guides all those who place their trust in Him.

Paris, 13 April [1620]

My dearest daughter,

Praise God who so far has guided you so well in these preliminary
steps toward your coming marriage! I hope this divine goodness will
give you complete peace. I must say, darling, that I myself am more and
more pleased about the match. In my opinion, M. de Toulonjon is as fine
a man as one could find anywhere. He has returned as happy as can be,
and we have every reason to feel the same. Truly, dear Françon, you have
pleased me very much by placing such total confidence in me; but if you
only knew how much I have prayed and longed to see you happily settled, and how much more keenly I feel your concerns than my own. Of

course, I shall always prefer your happiness to my own. There's no doubt about that. You may be sure that on this occasion I acted with great affection because I saw it was for your happiness. We owe everything to the goodness of our Lord who has watched over you and me and heard our prayers. You can see by the enclosed letter how much the Archbishop of Bourges wants this marriage also. So, stand fast if you are disturbed by fears and imaginings; shut the door upon them, and do not let such feelings enter, under any pretext whatever. In everything use common sense and follow my bit of advice. It is for your good, and if you continue to follow it, you will not regret it. Write me, as you have promised, all the feelings in your heart. And if, I hope, God Himself has bound you to M. de Toulonjon—for that is what I desire above all else— then I trust that God will have blessed your first meeting. For my part, darling, I tell you frankly, I find him altogether to my liking, as I have already said. Really, I like him very much. All our relatives and friends who know him couldn't ask for more.

As to your rings, M. de Toulonjon is very busy about them and wants to have lots of precious stones from Paris sent to me so that I may buy as many as I like for you. I would prefer that you not buy any at all, for, frankly, dear, ladies of rank here no longer wear them; only the townswomen do. However, you can make your own choice when you get here. But I don't know how to make M. de Toulonjon understand this, for he begs me, at least for now, to let him send you pearls, earrings, and a locket covered with diamonds, which is what all the ladies are wearing on the front of their gowns. Dearest, we mustn't let M. de Toulonjon be extravagant about buying so many things for you. He has such an intense desire to please you in every possible way, but we mustn't allow it. If ever there was a perfectly happy woman, it is you; but don't you see, dearest, you must be very discreet and hold him back in this. It will be better to put aside a little of your money and spend it more usefully than to squander it on such trinkets and vanities. For my part, I hope that my Françon will not be swept off her feet by all this. My reputation would be at stake, for since you are my daughter, you are expected to be circumspect and to conduct your affairs wisely and prudently.

I can just picture you as a lady, mistress of the heart and home of our very dear M. de Toulonjon! That's why it will be up to you to manage your affairs carefully. Since he wants you to send me a design of the dress you like, do so, but I am going to allow only one gown to be sent to you, for, more than one, considering all the other things he is getting for you, would be unreasonable. You yourself, if M. Coulon wants to help you, may also have one made, though I would prefer he simply send you the money for it. We could have it made in today's style and out of fashionable fabric so that it could be worn anywhere.

See to it that Foretz is sold. Moreover, you shouldn't have a wedding dress made; today that appears ridiculous among both the ladies at court and the gentry. Besides, I want you to have a quiet wedding; and I want you to trust me in this. M. de Toulonjon tells me that you don't want to be married in May. Good heavens! don't be scrupulous about this, for it's only a superstition. However, I don't think a May wedding is possible anyway, even though he would like that very much. That's because he wants to please you at any cost. I'd be in favor of a May wedding too if it meant your getting rid of your scruple about it. He wrote you about how he was prevented from coming here as soon as he had hoped, but he didn't tell you how he did get here. It happened that while he was waiting at the relay station, a friend of his, a State Councilor, was going by in his carriage. M. de Toulonjon jumped right into the carriage without his sword. He hadn't had time to eat but came just as he was. He was sorry not to have been able to send you anything today, but he will on Thursday. Really, the more I see this man, the more I like him and the more I realize how much you and I should praise God for this fortunate match. Write him a courteous, warm answer and speak honestly and openly with him, returning his affection. The time to stand on ceremony is over. His man is waiting downstairs for my letter. Dearest Françon, I want you to love your fiancé perfectly. May you be as happy as you have reason to be happy. As for me, I am completely happy, and with good reason. Goodbye, dearest love. Write to me quite openly.

P.S. A thousand greetings to our dear relatives. Goodbye again, darling. Let us love wholeheartedly him whom God has given us.

[Chambery, 1625]

Although I won't be seeing the Archbishop of Bourges as soon as we thought, still, I know my joy will be great when I do. Since his recovery and because of the graces our Lord has granted him, I feel extraordinary affection for him and I can't (nor do I want to) stop praising and thanking God for this great grace. He has written me nothing of what you tell me he did for my son, although he writes very often.[1] When I see him, I shall speak to him about this and I'll watch for an opportunity to put in a good word for you with him. I've always thought he was very fond of you, dearest. I don't think he owns much more than his furniture, but I really don't know. Darling, even if it were true that this good prelate had quite forgotten you, is that reason enough for you to give yourself over to sadness and resentment? Oh! Don't do that again; you might offend God. You are too attached to things of this life; you take them too much to heart.

What are you afraid of? That having many children you may not have the means of bringing them up in a style suited to their social background and to your courage? I beg you, don't worry about that. You underestimate the wise Providence of Him who gives you these children and who is good and rich enough to provide for them in a way befitting His glory and their salvation. This is what we should want for our children, rather than social ambition in this sad, mortal world.

And so, dearest, welcome very lovingly, as coming from the hand of God, these little ones that He gives you; take good care of them; cherish them tenderly, and bring them up in the fear of the Lord, and not in a spirit of vanity. If you do this, and if you entrust all your anxieties to God, you will see that His Providence looks after all your needs very nicely and that all you have to do is bless Him and rest in Him totally. Take my word for this, dearest. This is what you must do: serve God, let go of pride, live in harmony with the husband God has given you, take good care of your household; work at all this, and from now on, try to live like a real mother.

If I hadn't had the courage to do this at the beginning of my marriage, we would not have made ends meet for we had less income than you, and a debt of 15,000 crowns besides.

Courage, then, dearest; use your mind and your time, not to worry and fear, but to serve God and your household, for this is God's will for you. You will see how many blessings will flow from this undertaking.

I wanted to speak to you at length about all this. I hope that you will benefit from what I tell you with so much love and concern and that you

---

[1] Madame de Toulonjon was very hurt when she learned that her uncle, the Archbishop of Bourges, had favored her brother, the Baron de Chantal, in his will. By way of justifying her reaction, she wrote to her mother that her uncle had an obligation to provide for the future of his sister's children.

will reread this letter often so as to put it into practice. I ask God to grant
you this grace. In His goodness, may He shower His best blessings on
you and all your dear family whom I greet affectionately. You know, my
darling, that you are my one and only beloved, dearest daughter, and
that I am your very humble and very loving mother who wants you to
be completely happy.

[Annecy, 1626]

My dearest daughter,

I have just heard of the death of your son. May God, in His infinite
kindness, make up for your loss by filling you with an abundance of
spiritual and temporal graces! I am sure you have accepted this visitation from God with patience and a loving submission to his good pleasure, for in this valley of tears we must expect much sorrow and little
consolation. Raise your mind often to the thought of eternity, and aspire
to and long for this happiness. You will see that there is no real rest anywhere else; so love it and place all your hope in it. Teach this lesson early
to your little Gabrielle.

[Annecy, 1626]

My dearest daughter,

I hear God has blessed you with another pregnancy. I want to believe,
for my own consolation, that you are grateful for this grace, as well as for
all the prosperity you enjoy, and that you see all these gifts as coming
from the hand of God. He sends them to you, not for show, not to be
used out of vanity, but rather to help you advance in humility and a loving fear of Him from whom they come. Tell me frankly and truthfully,
dearest, where do you stand in this matter? I am always a little afraid that
the abundance of the advantages and honors of this world may obscure
your vision by their smoke, perhaps even choke you if you are not on
your guard or mindful of their inconstancy and the uncertainty of the
time of our departure from this life when we have to leave all that behind us. Think often of our passage from this life, my darling, and of the
eternity that awaits those who have valued lasting happiness more than
life's fleeting moments. Take care to impress these truths on your daughter's heart; this is the most valuable legacy you can obtain for her and be-
queath to her. Teach her to fear offending God and to value the happiness of living in love and fear of Him.

You know, darling, that ever since you were little I have tried to imprint this love of God on your heart and have always recommended that you obey His will, especially in rendering to your husband those duties required of you by God. I urge you to make him as happy as possible. Let me know also how you feel about this. Dearest, you shouldn't be solemn and pompous because of the wealth and honor that are yours. I'm told that you are becoming a scoffer. Believe me, dear, it would be better for you to attract attention by your modest, Christian manner and by the sweet and gracious affability you show everyone in your various relationships. Making fun of others is unbecoming in a woman of your social condition and age. Try to distinguish yourself and attract hearts by the means I have just mentioned. Above all, be prudent and reserved in your actions.

Receive this advice as coming from your mother who loves you dearly and who wants you always perfect in your state of life. God grant you this grace.

[Annecy, 1634][2]

I was deeply moved by your letter, my darling, which tells me how keenly you are suffering. Truly, your sorrow is great, and, when looked at only in terms of this earthly life, it is overwhelming. But if you can look beyond the ordinary and shifting events of life and consider the infinite blessings and consolations of eternity, you would find comfort in the midst of these reversals, as well as joy in the assured destiny of him for whom you mourn. Oh, when will we learn to be more attentive to these truths of our faith? When will we savor the tenderness of the Divine Will in all the events of our life, seeing in them only His good pleasure and His unchanging, mysterious love which is always concerned with our good, as much in prosperity as in adversity? But, imperfect as we are, we somehow transform into poison the very medicine the Great Physician prescribes for our healing. Let's stop behaving in such a manner. Rather, like obedient children, let's surrender ourselves lovingly to the will of our heavenly Father and cooperate with His plan to unite us intimately to Himself through suffering. If we do that, He will become all for us: our brother, son, husband, mother, our all in all. Courage! May you find strength in these thoughts.

---

[2] Françoise's husband, the Count de Toulonjon, died on September 20, 1633, the day she gave birth to a son. Now, in 1634, she is still grieving.

I beg our Lord to help you find the rich treasure which His Goodness has hidden at the very core of the pain that comes to you from His hand. [. . .]

My dearest,

You wanted to have my advice in writing, so here it is. My greatest wish is that you live like a true Christian widow, unpretentious in your dress and actions, and especially reserved in your relationships, having nothing to do with vain, worldly young men. Otherwise, dear, even though I am very sure that your conduct is above reproach—I feel more sure about it than of my own—others could question and criticize it if you entertained such persons in your house and took pleasure in their company. Please trust me in this, for your honor and mine, as well as for my peace of mind. I know very well, darling, of course, that we can't live in the world without enjoying some of its pleasures, but take my word for it, dearest, you won't find any really lasting joys except in God, in living virtuously, raising your children well, looking after their affairs and managing your household. If you seek happiness elsewhere, you will experience much anguish, as I well know.

I am not against the legitimate pleasure you can derive, by way of diversion, from healthy relationships with good people. But visits should be infrequent, considering the condition of life in which God has placed you. In other words, dearest, check your inclinations and surrender them to God for His glory dwelling in you, for the respect and love you owe to the memory of your beloved husband, the preservation of your good name, and the benefit of your daughter who, undoubtedly, will model herself after you. This surrender of your inclinations to God will be advantageous to you and to your dear children, and appropriate to your background, your present state in life and the consolation of your relatives. You will find strength to do this, darling, if you follow faithfully the little devotional practices we spoke of and which I shall now write out for you.

First, upon awakening in the morning, turn your thoughts to God present everywhere; place your heart and your entire being in His hands. Then think briefly of the good you will be able to accomplish that day and the evil you can avoid, especially by controlling your predominant fault. Resolve, by the grace of God, to do good and avoid evil. Then kneel down, adore God from the bottom of your heart and thank Him for all the benefits and graces He has given you. If you think about it for a moment, you will realize how He has surrounded you with His grace and taken special care of you. This thought should touch your heart which you ought to offer Him with all your good resolutions, affections, thoughts, words and deeds of that day, in union with our Divine Savior's offering of Himself on the tree of the cross. Ask Him for His grace and assistance to guide you throughout the day. Ask also for His blessing, that of the Blessed Virgin, your good angel and your patron saints by a simple turning to them in your heart. All this can be done in the space of two *Paters* and *Aves*; then get dressed quickly.

As far as possible, assist at Holy Mass every day as attentively and devoutly as possible, using such considerations as are given in *The Devout Life*. If you can't be present at Mass, at least be there in spirit, as suggested in the same book which ought to be your favorite spiritual guide.

Either during Mass, if you can't do otherwise, or at some other time in the morning, withdraw to some quiet place to pray from your heart for about a quarter of an hour. Place yourself before God or the Blessed Virgin, like a daughter in the presence of her father or mother, conversing with them with humble, filial trust, either by meditating on some mystery of faith, or else, following the promptings of your heart, by simply talking to them about the concerns you have right now. Always conclude your prayer with a strong desire to love and please God, renewing your good resolutions and asking for His grace. Above all, try to have a pure intention in all that you do; frequently offer your actions to God. Often call to mind His goodness and make loving aspirations, according to either His inspirations or the inclinations of your own heart.

Every day read for a quarter or half hour from some spiritual book, preferably from *Philothea*. Before supper, withdraw a bit, or while walking, place yourself in God's hands and make a few aspirations. Before going to bed, examine your conscience and, kneeling in God's presence, adore Him, thank Him, and offer Him your soul. If you can, add the litany of our Lady and have your servants answer the invocations. Receive holy communion at least on the first Sunday of each month, on the major feasts of our Lord and our Lady, and on the feast of Saint Joseph to whom I would like you to have devotion.

In conclusion, dear one, try to calm your passions and inclinations and live according to sound reason and the holy will of God. Otherwise, you will always be anxious and perturbed. But if you are fortunate enough to accept with patience and gentleness the sorrows and difficulties of this life, which God sends to those he loves for their growth and progress toward blessedness, then even in this life you will begin to get a little taste of the delights of a glorious eternity. You may be sure of this, darling. But you must sincerely turn to God and love Him in all the manifestations of His good pleasure. By obeying God's will, we prefer it to our own will, desires and inclinations. May God, in his kindness, grant us this grace, dearest. This is what I pray for constantly, for I love you so specially and with all my heart.

1. Describe Jane de Chantal's advice to her daughter before her daughter's marriage.
2. Was her daughter's marriage a happy one? Why or why not?
3. Did Jane de Chantal give good advice?

The Second Vatican Council

The Second Vatican Council (1962–1965) was a great event in the modern history of the Church. Scholars, theologians, and pastors continue to debate its meaning, but there is no doubting that its impact has been great. Promulgated at the last session of the Council, *Gaudium et Spes* belongs among the Council's most important documents. The excerpt below sets forth the Council's teaching about marriage and the family in the modern world.

Part II, Chapter I: Fostering the Nobility of Marriage and the Family

THE WELL-BEING OF THE INDIVIDUAL PERSON and of human and Christian society is intimately linked with the healthy condition of that community produced by marriage and family. Hence Christians and all men who hold this community in high esteem sincerely rejoice in the various ways by which men today find help in fostering this community of love and perfecting its life, and by which parents are assisted in their lofty calling. Those who rejoice in such aids look for additional benefits from them and labor to bring them about.

Yet the excellence of this institution is not everywhere reflected with equal brilliance, since polygamy, the plague of divorce, so-called free

---

From *Gaudium et Spes*, Pastoral Constitution on the Church in the Modern World (December 7, 1965, Second Vatican Council), paragraph nos. 47–52.

love and other disfigurements have an obscuring effect. In addition, married love is too often profaned by excessive self-love, the worship of pleasure and illicit practices against human generation. Moreover, serious disturbances are caused in families by modern economic conditions, by influences at once social and psychological, and by the demands of civil society. Finally, in certain parts of the world problems resulting from population growth are generating concern.

All these situations have produced anxiety of consciences. Yet, the power and strength of the institution of marriage and family can also be seen in the fact that time and again, despite the difficulties produced, the profound changes in modern society reveal the true character of this institution in one way or another.

Therefore, by presenting certain key points of Church doctrine in a clearer light, this sacred synod wishes to offer guidance and support to those Christians and other men who are trying to preserve the holiness and to foster the natural dignity of the married state and its superlative value.

The intimate partnership of married life and love has been established by the Creator and qualified by His laws, and is rooted in the conjugal covenant of irrevocable personal consent. Hence by that human act whereby spouses mutually bestow and accept each other a relationship arises which by divine will and in the eyes of society too is a lasting one. For the good of the spouses and their offsprings as well as of society, the existence of the sacred bond no longer depends on human decisions alone. For, God Himself is the author of matrimony, endowed as it is with various benefits and purposes. All of these have a very decisive bearing on the continuation of the human race, on the personal development and eternal destiny of the individual members of a family, and on the dignity, stability, peace and prosperity of the family itself and of human society as a whole. By their very nature, the institution of matrimony itself and conjugal love are ordained for the procreation and education of children, and find in them their ultimate crown. Thus a man and a woman, who by their compact of conjugal love "are no longer two, but one flesh" (Mt 19:6), render mutual help and service to each other through an intimate union of their persons and of their actions. Through this union they experience the meaning of their oneness and attain to it with growing perfection day by day. As a mutual gift of two persons, this intimate union and the good of the children impose total fidelity on the spouses and argue for an unbreakable oneness between them.

Christ the Lord abundantly blessed this many-faceted love, welling up as it does from the fountain of divine love and structured as it is on the model of His union with His Church. For as God of old made Himself present to His people through a covenant of love and fidelity, so now the Savior of men and the Spouse of the Church comes into the lives of married Christians through the sacrament of matrimony. He abides with them thereafter so that just as He loved the Church and handed Himself over on her behalf, the spouses may love each other with perpetual fidelity through mutual self-bestowal.

Authentic married love is caught up into divine love and is governed and enriched by Christ's redeeming power and the saving activity of the Church, so that this love may lead the spouses to God with powerful effect and may aid and strengthen them in sublime office of being a father or a mother. For this reason Christian spouses have a special sacrament by which they are fortified and receive a kind of consecration in the duties and dignity of their state. By virtue of this sacrament, as spouses fulfil their conjugal and family obligation, they are penetrated with the spirit of Christ, which suffuses their whole lives with faith, hope and charity. Thus they increasingly advance the perfection of their own personalities, as well as their mutual sanctification, and hence contribute jointly to the glory of God.

As a result, with their parents leading the way by example and family prayer, children and indeed everyone gathered around the family hearth will find a readier path to human maturity, salvation and holiness. Graced with the dignity and office of fatherhood and motherhood, parents will energetically acquit themselves of a duty which devolves primarily on them, namely education and especially religious education.

As living members of the family, children contribute in their own way to making their parents holy. For they will respond to the kindness of their parents with sentiments of gratitude, with love and trust. They will stand by them as children should when hardships overtake their parents and old age brings its loneliness. Widowhood, accepted bravely as a continuation of the marriage vocation, should be esteemed by all. Families too will share their spiritual riches generously with other families. Thus the Christian family, which springs from marriage as a reflection of the loving covenant uniting Christ with the Church, and as a participation in that covenant, will manifest to all men Christ's living presence in the world, and the genuine nature of the Church. This the family will do by the mutual love of the spouses, by their generous fruitfulness, their solidarity and faithfulness, and by the loving way in which all members of the family assist one another.

The biblical Word of God several times urges the betrothed and the married to nourish and develop their wedlock by pure conjugal love and undivided affection. Many men of our own age also highly regard true love between husband and wife as it manifests itself in a variety of ways depending on the worthy customs of various peoples and times.

This love is an eminently human one since it is directed from one person to another through an affection of the will; it involves the good of the whole person, and therefore can enrich the expressions of body and mind with a unique dignity, ennobling these expressions as special ingredients and signs of the friendship distinctive of marriage. This love God has judged worthy of special gifts, healing, perfecting and exalting gifts of grace and of charity. Such love, merging the human with the divine, leads the spouses to a free and mutual gift of themselves, a gift providing itself by gentle affection and by deed; such love pervades the whole of their lives: indeed by its busy generosity it grows better and grows greater. Therefore it far excels mere erotic inclination, which, selfishly pursued, soon enough fades wretchedly away.

This love is uniquely expressed and perfected through the appropriate enterprise of matrimony. The actions within marriage by which the couple are united intimately and chastely are noble and worthy ones. Expressed in a manner which is truly human, these actions promote that mutual self-giving by which spouses enrich each other with a joyful and a ready will. Sealed by mutual faithfulness and hallowed above all by Christ's sacrament, this love remains steadfastly true in body and in mind, in bright days or dark. It will never be profaned by adultery or divorce. Firmly established by the Lord, the unity of marriage will radiate from the equal personal dignity of wife and husband, a dignity acknowledged by mutual and total love. The constant fulfillment of the duties of this Christian vocation demands notable virtue. For this reason, strengthened by grace for holiness of life, the couple will painstakingly cultivate and pray for steadiness of love, large-heartedness and the spirit of sacrifice.

Authentic conjugal love will be more highly prized, and wholesome public opinion created about it if Christian couples give outstanding witness to faithfulness and harmony in their love, and to their concern for educating their children; also, if they do their part in bringing about the needed cultural, psychological and social renewal on behalf of marriage and the family. Especially in the heart of their own families, young people should be aptly and seasonably instructed in the dignity, duty and work of married love. Trained thus in the cultivation of chastity, they will be able at a suitable age to enter a marriage of their own after an honorable courtship.

Marriage and conjugal love are by their nature ordained toward the begetting and educating of children. Children are really the supreme gift of marriage and contribute very substantially to the welfare of their parents. The God Himself Who said, "it is not good for man to be alone" (Gen 2:18) and "Who made man from the beginning male and female" (Mt 19:4), wishing to share with man a certain special participation in His own creative work, blessed male and female, saying: "Increase and multiply" (Gen 1:28). Hence, while not making the other purposes of matrimony of less account, the true practice of conjugal love, and the whole meaning of the family life which results from it, have this aim: that the couple be ready with stout hearts to cooperate with the love of the Creator and the Savior, Who through them will enlarge and enrich His own family day by day.

Parents should regard as their proper mission the task of transmitting human life and educating those to whom it has been transmitted. They should realize that they are thereby cooperators with the love of God the Creator, and are, so to speak, the interpreters of that love. Thus they will fulfil their task with human and Christian responsibility, and, with docile reverence toward God, will make decisions by common counsel and effort. Let them thoughtfully take into account both their own welfare and that of their children, those already born and those which the future may bring. For this accounting they need to reckon with both the material and the spiritual conditions of the times as well as of their state in life. Finally, they should consult the interests of the family group, of temporal society, and of the Church herself. The parents themselves and no one else should ultimately make this judgment in the sight of God. But in their manner of acting, spouses should be aware that they cannot proceed arbitrarily, but must always be governed according to a conscience dutifully conformed to the divine law itself, and should be submissive toward the Church's teaching office, which authentically interprets that law in the light of the Gospel. That divine law reveals and protects the integral meaning of conjugal love, and impels it toward a truly human fulfilment. Thus, trusting in divine Providence and refining the spirit of sacrifice, married Christians glorify the Creator and strive toward fulfilment in Christ when with a generous human and Christian sense of responsibility they acquit themselves of the duty to procreate. Among the couples who fulfil their God-given task in this way, those merit special mention who with a gallant heart, and with wise and common deliberation, undertake to bring up suitably even a relatively large family.

Marriage to be sure is not instituted solely for procreation; rather, its very nature as an unbreakable compact between persons, and the welfare of the children, both demand that the mutual love of the spouses be embodied in a rightly ordered manner, that it grow and ripen. Therefore, marriage persists as a whole manner and communion of life, and maintains its value and indissolubility, even when despite the often intense desire of the couple, offspring are lacking.

This council realizes that certain modern conditions often keep couples from arranging their married lives harmoniously, and that they find themselves in circumstances where at least temporarily the size of their families should not be increased. As a result, the faithful exercise of love and the full intimacy of their lives is hard to maintain. But where the intimacy of married life is broken off, its faithfulness can sometimes be imperiled and its quality of fruitfulness ruined, for then the upbringing of the children and the courage to accept new ones are both endangered.

To these problems there are those who presume to offer dishonorable solutions indeed; they do not recoil even from the taking of life. But the Church issues the reminder that a true contradiction cannot exist between the divine laws pertaining to the transmission of life and those pertaining to authentic conjugal love.

For God, the Lord of life, has conferred on men the surpassing ministry of safeguarding life in a manner which is worthy of man. Therefore from the moment of its conception life must be guarded with the greatest care while abortion and infanticide are unspeakable crimes. The sexual characteristics of man and the human faculty of reproduction wonderfully exceed the dispositions of lower forms of life. Hence the acts themselves which are proper to conjugal love and which are exercised in accord with genuine human dignity must be honored with great reverence. Hence when there is question of harmonizing conjugal love with the responsible transmission of life, the moral aspects of any procedure does not depend solely on sincere intentions or on an evaluation of motives, but must be determined by objective standards. These, based on the nature of the human person and his acts, preserve the full sense of mutual self-giving and human procreation in the context of true love. Such a goal cannot be achieved unless the virtue of conjugal chastity is sincerely practiced. Relying on these principles, sons of the Church may not undertake methods of birth control which are found blameworthy by the teaching authority of the Church in its unfolding of the divine law.

All should be persuaded that human life and the task of transmitting it are not realities bound up with this world alone. Hence they cannot be measured or perceived only in terms of it, but always have a bearing on the eternal destiny of men.

The family is a kind of school of deeper humanity. But if it is to achieve the full flowering of its life and mission, it needs the kindly communion of minds and the joint deliberation of spouses, as well as the painstaking cooperation of parents in the education of their children. The active presence of the father is highly beneficial to their formation. The children, especially the younger among them, need the care of their mother at home. This domestic role of hers must be safely preserved, though the legitimate social progress of women should not be underrated on that account.

Children should be so educated that as adults they can follow their vocation, including a religious one, with a mature sense of responsibility and can choose their state of life; if they marry, they can thereby establish their family in favorable moral, social and economic conditions. Parents or guardians should by prudent advice provide guidance to their young with respect to founding a family, and the young ought to listen gladly. At the same time no pressure, direct or indirect, should be put on the young to make them enter marriage or choose a specific partner.

Thus the family, in which the various generations come together and help one another grow wiser and harmonize personal rights with the other requirements of social life, is the foundation of society. All those, therefore, who exercise influence over communities and social groups should work efficiently for the welfare of marriage and the family. Public authority should regard it as a sacred duty to recognize, protect and promote their authentic nature, to shield public morality and to favor the prosperity of home life. The right of parents to beget and educate their children in the bosom of the family must be safeguarded. Children too who unhappily lack the blessing of a family should be protected by prudent legislation and various undertakings and assisted by the help they need.

Christians, redeeming the present time and distinguishing eternal realities from their changing expressions, should actively promote the values of marriage and the family, both by the examples of their own lives and by cooperation with other men of good will. Thus when difficulties arise, Christians will provide, on behalf of family life, those necessities and helps which are suitably modern. To this end, the Christian instincts of the faithful, the upright moral consciences of men, and the wisdom and experience of persons versed in the sacred sciences will have much to contribute.

Those too who are skilled in other sciences, notably the medical, biological, social and psychological, can considerably advance the welfare of marriage and the family along with peace of conscience if by pooling their efforts they labor to explain more thoroughly the various conditions favoring a proper regulation of births.

It devolves on priests duly trained about family matters to nurture the vocation of spouses by a variety of pastoral means, by preaching God's word, by liturgical worship, and by other spiritual aids to conjugal and family life; to sustain them sympathetically and patiently in difficulties, and to make them courageous through love, so that families which are truly illustrious can be formed.

Various organizations, especially family associations, should try by their programs of instruction and action to strengthen young people and spouses themselves, particularly those recently wed, and to train them for family, social and apostolic life.

Finally, let the spouses themselves, made to the image of the living God and enjoying the authentic dignity of persons, be joined to one another in equal affection, harmony of mind and the work of mutual sanctification. Thus, following Christ who is the principle of life, by the sacrifices and joys of their vocation and through their faithful love, married people can become witnesses of the mystery of love which the Lord revealed to the world by His dying and His rising up to life again.

1. Why does *Gaudium et Spes* concern itself with marriage and the family?
2. Does *Gaudium et Spes*, written in 1965, continue to speak to contemporary problems?
3. How does *Gaudium et Spes* describe the purposes of marriage and family life?

Pope John Paul II

Born in 1920 in Poland, Karol Wojtyla was elected pope and took the name John Paul II in 1978. An accomplished philosopher, poet, and playwright, Pope John Paul II had devoted much of his philosophical career to the topic of personhood and to sexual ethics, set forth in particular in his philosophical study *Love and Responsibility* (1960). After becoming pope, he began using his weekly "general audiences" to deliver a series of talks on what he termed the "theology of the body," in which, drawing upon the book of Genesis, he argues that the complementary bodies of male and female persons manifest the human person's vocation to the radical gift of self. Lust distorts the gift of self by treating sexuality as a matter of using the other person as an instrumental means to an end.

The Relationship of Lust to the Communion of Persons

General audience of June 4, 1980

Speaking of the birth of lust, on the basis of the Book of Genesis, we analyzed the original meaning of shame, which appeared with the first sin. The analysis of shame, in the light of the biblical narrative, enables us to understand even more thoroughly the meaning it has for interpersonal

From *Blessed Are the Pure of Heart* (Boston, Mass.: St. Paul Books & Media, 1983), 55–78; see also *The Theology of the Body* (Boston: St. Paul Books & Media, 1997), 117–127.

man-woman relations as a whole. The third chapter of Genesis shows without any doubt that that shame appeared in man's mutual relationship with woman and that this relationship, by reason of the very shame itself, underwent a radical transformation. Since it was born in their hearts together with the lust of the body, the analysis of original shame enables us at the same time to examine in what relationship this lust remains with regard to the communion of persons, which was granted and assigned from the beginning as the man and woman's task owing to the fact that they had been created "in the image of God." Therefore, the further stage of the study of lust, which had been manifested "at the beginning" through the man and woman's shame, according to Genesis 3, is the analysis of the insatiability of the union, that is, of the communion of persons, which was to be expressed also by their bodies, according to their specific masculinity and femininity.

Above all, therefore, this shame, which, according to the biblical narrative, induces man and woman to hide from each other their bodies and particularly their sexual differentiation, confirms that the original capacity of communicating themselves to each other, of which Genesis 2:25 speaks, has been shattered. The radical change of the meaning of original nakedness leads us to presume negative changes in the whole interpersonal man-woman relationship. That mutual communion in humanity itself by means of the body and by means of its masculinity and femininity, which resounded so strongly in the preceding passage of the Yahwist narrative (cf. Gen 2:23–25), is upset at this moment: as if the body, in its masculinity and femininity, no longer constituted the "trustworthy" substratum of the communion of persons, as if its original function were "called in question" in the consciousness of man and woman.

The simplicity and "purity" of the original experience, which facilitated an extraordinary fullness in the mutual communication of each other, disappear. Obviously, our first progenitors did not stop communicating with each other through the body and its movements, gestures and expressions; but the simple and direct communion with each other, connected with the original experience of reciprocal nakedness, disappeared. Almost unexpectedly, there appeared in their consciousness an insuperable threshold, which limited the original "giving of oneself" to the other, in full confidence in what constituted their own identity and, at the same time, their diversity, female on the one side, male on the other. The diversity, that is, the difference of the male sex and the female sex, was suddenly felt and understood as an element of mutual confrontation of persons. This is testified to by the concise expression of Genesis 3:7, "They knew that they were naked," and by its immediate context. All that is part also of the analysis of the first shame. The Book of Genesis not only portrays its origin in the human being, but makes it possible also to reveal its degrees in both, man and woman.

The ending of the capacity of a full mutual communion, which is manifested as sexual shame, enables us to understand better the original value of the unifying meaning of the body. It is not possible, in fact, to understand otherwise that respective closure to each other, or shame, unless in relation to the meaning that the body, in its femininity and masculinity, had for man previously, in the state of original innocence. That unifying meaning is understood not only with regard to the unity that man and woman, as spouses, were to constitute, becoming "one flesh" (Gen 2:24) through the conjugal act, but also in reference to the "communion of persons" itself, which had been the specific dimension of man and woman's existence in the mystery of creation. The body in its masculinity and femininity constituted the peculiar "substratum" of this personal communion. Sexual shame, with which Genesis 3:7 deals, bears witness to the loss of the original certainty that the human body, through its masculinity and femininity, is precisely that "substratum" of the communion of persons, that expresses it "simply," that it serves the purpose of realizing it (and thus also of completing the "image of God" in the visible world).

This state of consciousness in both has strong repercussions in the further context of Genesis 3, with which we shall deal shortly. If man, after original sin, had lost, so to speak, the sense of the image of God in himself, that loss was manifested with shame of the body (cf. particularly Gen 3:10–11). That shame, encroaching upon the man-woman relationship in its totality, was manifested with the imbalance of the original meaning of corporeal unity, that is, of the body as the peculiar "substratum" of the communion of persons. As if the personal profile of masculinity and femininity, which, before, highlighted the meaning of the body for a full communion of persons, had made way only for the sensation of "sexuality" with regard to the other human being. And as if sexuality became an "obstacle" in the personal relationship of man and woman. Concealing it from each other, according to Genesis 3:7, they both express it almost instinctively.

This is, at the same time, the "second" discovery of sex, as it were, which in the biblical narrative differs radically from the first one. The whole context of the narrative confirms that this new discovery distinguishes "historical" man with his lust (with the three forms of lust, in fact) from man of original innocence. What is the relationship of lust, and in particular the lust of the flesh, with regard to the communion of persons mediated by the body, by its masculinity and femininity, that is, to the communion assigned, "from the beginning" to man by the Creator? This is the question that must be posed, precisely with regard "to the beginning," about the experience of shame, to which the biblical narrative refers.

Shame, as we have already observed, is manifested in the narrative of Genesis 3 as a symptom of man's detachment from the love in which he participated in the mystery of creation according to the Johannine expression: the love that "comes from the Father." "The love that is in the world," that is, lust, brings with it an almost constitutive difficulty of identification with one's own body: and not only in the sphere of one's own subjectivity, but even more with regard to the subjectivity of the other human being: of woman for man, of man for woman.

Hence the necessity of hiding before the "other" with one's own body, with what determines one's own femininity-masculinity. This necessity proves the fundamental lack of trust, which in itself indicates the collapse of the original relationship "of communion." Precisely regard for the subjectivity of the other, and at the same time for one's own subjectivity, has aroused in this new situation, that is, in the context of lust, the necessity of hiding oneself, of which Genesis 3:7 speaks.

Precisely here it seems to us that we can discover a deeper meaning of "sexual" shame and also the full meaning of that phenomenon, to which the biblical text refers, to point out the boundary between the man of original innocence and the "historical" man of lust. The complete text of Genesis 3 supplies us with elements to define the deepest dimension of shame; but that calls for a separate analysis. We will begin it in the next reflection.

Dominion over the Other in the Interpersonal Relation

General audience of June 18, 1980

The phenomenon of shame, which appeared in the first man together with original sin, is described with surprising precision in Genesis 3.

Careful reflection on this text enables us to deduce from it that shame, which took the place of the absolute trust connected with the previous state of original innocence in the mutual relationship between man and woman, has a deeper dimension. In this connection it is necessary to reread chapter 3 of Genesis to the end, and not limit ourselves to verse 7 or the text of verses 10–11, which contain the testimony about the first experience of shame. After this narrative, the dialogue of God-Yahweh with the man and the woman breaks off and a monologue begins. Yahweh turns to the woman and speaks first of the pain of childbirth, which will accompany her from now on: "I will greatly multiply your pain in childbearing; in pain you shall bring forth children . . ." (Gen 3:16).

That is followed by the expression which characterizes the future relationship of both, of the man and the woman: "your desire shall be for your husband, and he shall rule over you" (Gen 3:16).

These words, like those of Genesis 2:24, have a perspective character. The incisive formulation of 3:16 seems to regard the facts as a whole, which have already emerged, in a way, in the original experience of shame, and which will subsequently be manifested in the whole interior experience of "historical" man. The history of consciences and of human hearts will contain the continual confirmation of the words contained in Genesis 3:16. The words spoken at the beginning seem to refer to a particular "disability" of woman as compared with man. But there is no reason to understand it as a social disability or inequality. The expression: "your desire shall be for your husband, and he shall rule over you" immediately indicates, on the other hand, another form of inequality, which woman will feel as a lack of full unity precisely in the vast context of union with man, to which both were called according to Genesis 2:24.

The words of God-Yahweh: "your desire shall be for your husband, and he shall rule over you" (Gen 3:16), do not concern exclusively the moment of man and woman's union, when both unite in such a way as to become one flesh (cf. Gen 2:24), but refer to the ample context of relations, also indirect ones, of conjugal union as a whole. For the first time the man is defined here as "husband." In the whole context of the Yahwist narrative these words mean above all, a violation, a fundamental loss, of the original community-communion of persons. The latter should have made man and woman mutually happy by means of the pursuit of a simple and pure union in humanity, by means of a reciprocal offering of themselves, that is, the experience of the gift of the person expressed with the soul and with the body, with masculinity and femininity ("flesh of my flesh": Gen 2:23), and finally by means of the subordination of this union to the blessing of fertility with "procreation."

It seems, therefore, that in the words addressed by God-Yahweh to the woman, there is a deeper echo of the shame, which they both began to experience after the breaking of the original covenant with God. We find, moreover, a fuller motivation of this shame. In a very discreet way, which is, nevertheless, decipherable and expressive, Genesis 3:16 testifies how that original beatifying conjugal union of persons will be distorted in man's heart by lust. These words are addressed directly to woman, but they refer to man, or rather to both together.

The previous analysis of Genesis 3:7 already showed that in the new situation, after the breaking of the original covenant with God, the man and the woman found themselves, instead of united, more divided or even opposed because of their masculinity and femininity. The biblical narrative, stressing the instinctive impulse that had driven them both to cover their bodies, describes at the same time the situation in which man, as male *or* female—before it was rather male *and* female—feels more estranged from the body, as from the source of the original union in humanity ("flesh of my flesh"), and more opposed to the other precisely on the basis of the body and sex. This opposition does not destroy or exclude conjugal union, willed by the Creator (cf. Gen 2:24), or its procreative effects; but it confers on the realization of this union another direction, which will be precisely that of the man of lust. Genesis 3:16 speaks precisely of this.

The woman, whose "desire shall be for [her] husband" (cf. Gen 3:16), and the man who responds to this desire, as we read: "shall rule over you," unquestionably form the same human couple, the same marriage as Genesis 2:24, in fact, the same community of persons; however, they are now something different. They are no longer called only to union and unity, but also threatened by the insatiability of that union and unity, which does not cease to attract man and woman precisely because they are persons, called from eternity to exist "in communion." In the light of the biblical narrative, sexual shame has its deep meaning, which is connected precisely with the failure to satisfy the aspiration to realize in the "conjugal union of the body" (cf. Gen 2:24) the mutual communion of persons.

All that seems to confirm, from various aspects, that at the basis of shame, in which "historical" man has become a participant, there is the threefold lust spoken of in the First Letter of John 2:16: not only the lust of the flesh, but also "the lust of the eyes and the pride of life." Does not the expression regarding "rule" ("he shall rule over you"), of which we read in Genesis 3:16, indicate this last form of lust? Does not the rule "over" the other—of man over woman—change essentially the structure of communion in the interpersonal relationship? Does it not transpose into the dimension of this structure something that makes the human being an object, which can, in a way, be desired by the lust of the eyes?

These are the questions that spring from reflection on the words of God-Yahweh according to Genesis 3:16. Those words, delivered almost on the threshold of human history after original sin, reveal to us not only the exterior situation of man and woman, but enable us also to penetrate into the deep mysteries of their hearts.

Lust Limits the Nuptial Meaning of the Body

General audience of June 25, 1980

The analysis we made during the preceding reflection was centered on the following words of Genesis 3:16, addressed by God-Yahweh to the first woman after original sin: "your desire shall be for your husband, and he shall rule over you" (Gen 3:16). We arrived at the conclusion that these words contain an adequate clarification and a deep interpretation of original shame (cf. Gen 3:7), which became part of man and of woman together with lust. The explanation of this shame is not to be sought in the body itself, in the somatic sexuality of both, but goes back to the deeper changes undergone by the human spirit. Precisely this spirit is particularly aware of how insatiable it is with regard to the mutual unity between man and woman.

This awareness, so to speak, blames the body, and deprives it of the simplicity and purity of the meaning connected with the original innocence of the human being. In relation to this awareness, shame is a secondary experience. If on the one hand it reveals the moment of lust, at the same time it can protect from the consequences of the three forms of lust. It can even be said that man and woman, through shame, almost remain in the state of original innocence. Continually, in fact, they become aware of the nuptial meaning of the body and aim at preserving it, so to speak, from lust, just as they try to maintain the value of communion, that is, of the union of persons in the "unity of the body."

Genesis 2:24 speaks with discretion but also with clarity of the "union of bodies" in the sense of the authentic union of persons: "A man . . . cleaves to his wife, and they become one flesh"; and it is seen from the context that this union comes from a choice, since the man "leaves" his father and mother to unite with his wife. Such a union of persons entails that they should become "one flesh." Starting from this "sacramental" expression, which corresponds to the communion of persons—of the man and the woman—in their original call to conjugal union, we can understand better the specific message of Genesis 3:16; that is, we can establish and, as it were, reconstruct what the imbalance, in fact, the peculiar distortion of the original interpersonal relationship of communion, to which the "sacramental" words of Genesis 2:24 refer, consists of.

It can therefore be said—studying Genesis 3:16—that while on the one hand the "body," constituted in the unity of the personal subject, does not cease to stimulate the desires of personal union, precisely because of masculinity and femininity ("your desire shall be for your husband"), on the other hand and at the same time, lust directs these desires in its own way. That is confirmed by the expression: "he shall rule over you."

The lust of the flesh directs these desires, however, to satisfaction of the body, often at the cost of a real and full communion of persons. In this sense, attention should be paid to the way in which semantic accentuations are distributed in the verses of Genesis 3; in fact, although there are few of them, they reveal interior consistency. The man is the one who seems to feel ashamed of his own body with particular intensity: "I was afraid, because I was naked; and I hid myself" (Gen 3:10). These words emphasize the really metaphysical character of shame. At the same time, the man is the one for whom shame, united with lust, will become an impulse to "dominate" the woman ("he shall rule over you").

Subsequently, the experience of this domination is manifested more directly in the woman as the insatiable desire for a different union. From the moment when the man "dominates" her, the communion of persons—made of the full spiritual union of the two subjects giving

themselves to each other—is followed by a different mutual relationship, that is, the relationship of possession of the other as the object of
one's own desire. If this impulse prevails on the part of the man, the instincts that the woman directs to him, according to the expression of
Genesis 3:16, can—and do—assume a similar character. And sometimes, perhaps, they precede the man's "desire," or even aim at arousing
it and giving it impetus.

The text of Genesis 3:16 seems to indicate the man particularly as
the one who "desires," similarly to the text of Matthew 5:27–28, which
is the starting point of these meditations. Nevertheless, both the man
and the woman have become a "human being" subject to lust. And
therefore the lot of both is shame, which with its deep resonance
touches the innermost recesses both of the male and of the female personality, even though in a different way. What we learn from Genesis 3
enables us barely to outline this duality, but even the mere references
are already very significant. Let us add that, since it is a question of
such an archaic text, it is surprisingly eloquent and acute.

An adequate analysis of Genesis 3 leads therefore to the conclusion
that the three forms of lust, including that of the body, bring with them
a limitation of the nuptial meaning of the body itself, in which man and
woman participated in the state of original innocence. When we speak
of the meaning of the body, we refer in the first place to the full awareness of the human being, but we also include all actual experience of the
body in its masculinity and femininity, and, in any case, the constant
predisposition to this experience.

The "meaning" of the body is not just something conceptual. We have
already drawn attention to this sufficiently in the preceding analyses.
The "meaning of the body" is at the same time what determines the
attitude: it is the way of living the body. It is a measure which the interior man, that is, that "heart" to which Christ refers in the Sermon on
the Mount, applies to the human body with regard to his masculinity/
femininity (therefore with regard to his sexuality).

That "meaning" does not change the reality in itself, that which the
human body is and does not cease to be in the sexuality that is characteristic of it, independently of the states of our conscience and our experiences. However, this purely objective significance of the body and
of sex, outside the system of real and concrete interpersonal relations
between man and woman, is, in a certain sense, "a-historical." In the

present analysis, on the contrary—in conformity with the biblical sources—we always take man's historicity into account (also because of the fact that we start from his theological prehistory). It is a question here, obviously, of an interior dimension, which eludes the external criteria of historicity, but which, however, can be considered "historical." In fact, it is precisely at the basis of all the facts which constitute the history of man—also the history of sin and of salvation—and thus reveal the depth and very root of his historicity.

When, in this vast context, we speak of lust as limitation, infraction or even distortion of the nuptial meaning of the body, we are referring above all to the preceding analyses regarding the state of original innocence, that is, the theological prehistory of man. At the same time, we have in mind the measure that "historical" man, with his "heart," applies to his own body in relation to male/female sexuality. This measure is not something exclusively conceptual: it is what determines the attitudes and decides in general the way of living the body.

Certainly, Christ refers to that in His Sermon on the Mount. We are trying here to link up the words taken from Matthew 5:27–28 to the very threshold of man's theological history, taking them, therefore, into consideration already in the context of Genesis 3. Lust as limitation, infraction or even distortion of the nuptial meaning of the body can be ascertained in a particularly clear way (in spite of the concise nature of the biblical narrative) in our first progenitors, Adam and Eve. Thanks to them we have been able to find the nuptial meaning of the body and rediscover what it consists of as a measure of the human "heart," such as to mold the original form of the communion of persons. If in their personal experience (which the biblical text enables us to follow) that original form *has undergone imbalance and distortion*—as we have sought to prove through the analysis of shame—*also the nuptial meaning of the body, which in the situation of original innocence constituted the measure of the heart of both, of the man and of the woman, must have undergone a distortion.* If we succeed in reconstructing in what this distortion consists, we shall also have the answer to our question: that is, what lust of the flesh consists of and what constitutes its theological and at the same time anthropological specific character. It seems that an answer theologically and anthropologically adequate—important as regards the meaning of Christ's words in the Sermon on the Mount (Mt 5:27–28)—can already be obtained from the context of Genesis 3 and from the whole Yahwist narrative, which previously enabled us to clarify the nuptial meaning of the human body.

The Heart—A Battlefield between Love and Lust

General audience of July 23, 1980

The human body in its original masculinity and femininity according to the mystery of creation—as we know from the analysis of Genesis 2:23–25—is not only a source of fertility, that is, of procreation, but right "from the beginning" has a nuptial character: that is to say, it is capable of expressing the love with which the man-person becomes a gift, thus fulfilling the deep meaning of his being and his existence. In this peculiarity, the body is the expression of the spirit and is called, in the very mystery of creation, to exist in the communion of persons "in the image of God." Well, the concupiscence "that comes from the world"— here it is a question of the concupiscence of the body—limits and distorts the body's objective way of existing, of which man has become a participant.

The human "heart" experiences the degree of this limitation or distortion, especially in the sphere of man-woman mutual relations. Precisely in the experience of the "heart" femininity and masculinity, in their mutual relations, no longer seem to be the expression of the spirit which aims at personal communion, and remain only an object of attraction, in a certain sense as happens "in the world" of living beings, which, like man, have received the blessing of fertility (cf. Gen 1).

This similarity is certainly contained in the work of creation; also Genesis 2 and particularly verse 24 confirm this. However, already in the mystery of creation, that which constituted the "natural," somatic and sexual substratum of that attraction, fully expressed the call of man and woman to personal communion. After sin, on the contrary, in the new situation of which Genesis 3 speaks, this expression was weakened and dimmed: as if it were lacking in the shaping of mutual relations, or as if it were driven back to another plane.

The natural and somatic substratum of human sexuality was manifested as an almost autogenous force, marked by a certain "coercion of the body," operating according to its own dynamics, which limits the expression of the spirit and the experience of the exchange of the gift of the person. The words of Genesis 3:15 addressed to the first woman seem to indicate this quite clearly ("your desire shall be for your husband, and he shall rule over you").

The human body in its masculinity/femininity has almost lost the capacity of expressing this love, in which the man-person becomes a gift, in conformity with the deepest structure and finality of his personal existence, as we have already observed in preceding analyses. If here we do not formulate this judgment absolutely and add the adverbial expression "almost," we do so because the dimension of the gift—namely, the capacity of expressing love with which man, by means of femininity and masculinity, becomes a gift for the other—continued to some extent to permeate and mold the love that is born in the human heart. The nuptial meaning of the body has not become completely suffocated by concupiscence, but only habitually threatened.

The "heart" has become a battlefield between love and lust. The more lust dominates the heart, the less the latter experiences the nuptial meaning of the body, and the less it becomes sensitive to the gift of the person, which, in the mutual relations of man and of woman expresses precisely that meaning. Certainly, that "lust" also of which Christ speaks in Matthew 5:27–28, appears in many forms in the human heart: it is not always plain and obvious; sometimes it is concealed, so that it passes itself off as "love," although it changes its true profile and dims the limpidity of the gift in the mutual relationship of persons. Does this mean that it is our duty to distrust the human heart? No! It only means that we must keep it under control.

The image of the concupiscence of the body, which emerges from the present analysis, has a clear reference to the image of the person, with which we connected our preceding reflections on the subject of the nuptial meaning of the body. Man, indeed, as a person is "the only creature on earth that God has willed for its own sake" and, at the same time, he is the one who "can fully discover his true self only in a sincere giving of himself."[1] Lust in general—and the lust of the body in particular—

---

[1] *Gaudium et spes*, no. 24: "Furthermore, the Lord Jesus, when praying to the Father 'that they may all be one . . . even as we are one' (Jn 17:21–22), has opened up new horizons closed to human reason by implying that there is a certain parallel between the union existing among the Divine Persons and the union of the sons of God in truth and love. It follows, then, that if man is the only creature on earth that God has willed for its own sake, man can fully discover his true self only in a sincere giving of himself."

attacks precisely this "sincere giving." It deprives man, it could be said, of the dignity of giving, which is expressed by his body through femininity and masculinity, and in a way it "depersonalizes" man making him an object "for the other." Instead of being "together with the other"—a subject in unity, in fact, in the sacramental unity "of the body"—man becomes an object for man: the female for the male and vice versa. The words of Genesis 3:16—and, even before, of Genesis 3:7—bear witness to this, with all the clearness of the contrast, as compared with Genesis 2:23–25.

Violating the dimension of the mutual giving of the man and the woman, concupiscence also calls in question the fact that each of them was willed by the Creator "for his own sake." The subjectivity of the person gives way, in a certain sense, to the objectivity of the body. Owing to the body, man becomes an object for man—the female for the male and vice versa. Concupiscence means, so to speak, that the personal relations of man and of woman are unilaterally and reductively linked with the body and sex, in the sense that these relations become almost incapable of accepting the mutual gift of the person. They do not contain or deal with femininity/masculinity according to the full dimension of personal subjectivity; they are not the expression of communion, but they remain unilaterally determined "by sex."

Concupiscence entails the loss of the interior freedom of the gift. The nuptial meaning of the human body is connected precisely with this freedom. Man can become a gift—that is, the man and the woman can exist in the relationship of mutual self-giving, if each of them controls himself. Concupiscence, which is manifested as a "coercion *sui generis* of the body," limits interiorly and reduces self-control, and for that reason, makes impossible, in a certain sense, the interior freedom of giving. Together with that, also the beauty that the human body possesses in its male and female aspect, as an expression of the spirit, is obscured. There remains the body as an object of lust and, therefore, as a "field of appropriation" of the other human being. Concupiscence, in itself, is not capable of promoting union as the communion of persons. By itself, it does not unite, but appropriates. The relationship of the gift is changed into the relationship of appropriation.

At this point, let us interrupt out reflections today. The last problem dealt with here is of such great importance, and is, moreover, so subtle, from the point of view of the difference between authentic love (that is,

between the "communion of persons") and lust, that we shall have to
take it up again at our next meeting.

1. What is wrong with lust or "concupiscence"?
2. What is the "nuptial meaning of the body"?
3. Describe the goal of "communion of persons."

Blessed Teresa of Calcutta

Blessed Teresa of Calcutta (1910–1997), widely known as Mother Teresa, was born into an ethnic Albanian peasant family in the former Yugoslavia. After entering religious life at age eighteen and becoming a teacher at the Loreto convent school in Calcutta, India, she founded the Missionaries of Charity in 1948 and began a life dedicated to the "poorest of the poor." Her work for the poor earned her a number of international prizes, including the Nobel Peace Prize, but she never ceased to challenge the world to live according to Christ's radically self-giving love and to value people rather than things. She delivered the following speech to an audience composed of the leading figures in American political life, including the President of the United States.

ON THE LAST DAY, JESUS WILL SAY TO THOSE on His right hand, "Come, enter the kingdom. For I was hungry and you gave me food, I was thirsty and you gave me drink, I was sick and you visited me." Then Jesus will turn to those on His left hand and say, "Depart from me because I was hungry and you did not feed me, I was thirsty, and you did not give me to drink, I was sick and you did not visit me." These will ask Him, "When did we see you hungry, or thirsty or sick and did not come to your help?" And Jesus will answer them, "Whatever you neglected to do unto one of the least of these, you neglected to do unto me!"

"Address to the National Prayer Breakfast" (Washington, D.C., February 3, 1994), published in *Crisis*, March 1994, 17–19. Reprinted with permission from *Crisis* magazine.

As we have gathered here to pray together, I think it will be beautiful if we begin with a prayer that expresses very well what Jesus wants us to do for the least. Saint Francis of Assisi understood very well these words of Jesus, and his life is very well expressed by a prayer. And this prayer, which we say every day after holy communion, always surprises me very much because it is very fitting for each one of us. And I always wonder whether 800 years ago when Saint Francis lived they had the same difficulties that we have today. I think that some of you already have this prayer of peace—so we will pray it together.

Let us thank God for the opportunity He has given us today to have come here to pray together. We have come here especially to pray for peace, joy and love. We are reminded that Jesus came to bring the good news to the poor. He had told us what is that good news when He said: "My peace I leave with you, My peace I give unto you." He came not to give the peace of the world which is only that we don't bother each other. He came to give the peace of heart which comes from loving—from doing good to others.

And God loved the world so much that He gave His son—it was a giving. God gave His son to the Virgin Mary, and what did she do with Him? As soon as Jesus came into Mary's life, immediately she went in haste to give that good news. And as she came into the house of her cousin, Elizabeth, Scripture tells us that the unborn child—the child in the womb of Elizabeth—leapt with joy. While still in the womb of Mary—Jesus brought peace to John the Baptist who leapt for joy in the womb of Elizabeth.

And as if that were not enough, as if it were not enough that God the Son should become one of us and bring peace and joy while still in the womb of Mary, Jesus also died on the Cross to show that greater love. He died for you and for me, and for that leper and for that man dying of hunger and that naked person lying in the street, not only of Calcutta, but of Africa, and everywhere. Our Sisters serve these poor people in 105 countries throughout the world. Jesus insisted that we love one another as He loves each one of us. Jesus gave His life to love us and He tells us that we also have to give whatever it takes to do good to one another. And in the Gospel Jesus says very clearly: "Love as I have loved you."

Jesus died on the Cross because that is what it took for Him to do good to us—to save us from our selfishness in sin. He gave up everything to do the Father's will—to show us that we too must be willing to give up everything to do God's will—to love one another as He loves each of us. If we are not willing to give whatever it takes to do good to one another, sin is still in us. That is why we too must give to each other until it hurts.

It is not enough for us to say: "I love God," but I also have to love my neighbor. Saint John says that you are a liar if you say you love God and you don't love your neighbor. How can you love God whom you do not see, if you do not love your neighbor whom you see, whom you touch, with whom you live? And so it is very important for us to realize that love, to be true, had to hurt. I must be willing to give whatever it takes not to harm other people and, in fact, to do good to them. This requires that I be willing to give until it hurts. Otherwise, there is no true love in me and I bring injustice, not peace, to those around me.

It hurt Jesus to love us. We have been created in His image for greater things, to love and to be loved. We must "put on Christ" as Scripture tells us. And so, we have been created to love as He loves us. Jesus makes Himself the hungry one, the naked one, the homeless one, the unwanted one, and He says, "You did it to Me." On the last day He will say to those on His right, "whatever you did to the least of these, you did to Me," and He will also say to those on His left, "whatever you neglected to do for the least of these, you neglected to do it for Me."

When He was dying on the Cross, Jesus said, "I thirst." Jesus is thirsting for our love, and this is the thirst of everyone, poor and rich alike. We all thirst for the love of others, that they go out of their way to avoid harming us and to do good to us. This is the meaning of true love, to give until it hurts.

I can never forget the experience I had in visiting a home where they kept all these old parents of sons and daughters who had just put them into an institution and forgotten them—maybe. I saw that in that home these old people had everything—good food, comfortable place, television, everything, but everyone was looking toward the door. And I did not see a single one with a smile on his face. I turned to Sister and I asked: "Why do these people who have every comfort here, why are they all looking toward the door? Why are they not smiling?"

I am so used to seeing the smiles on our people, even the dying ones smile. And Sister said: "This is the way it is nearly every day. They are expecting, they are hoping that a son or daughter will come to visit them.

They are hurt because they are forgotten." And see, this neglect to love brings spiritual poverty. Maybe in our own family we have somebody who is feeling lonely, who is feeling sick, who is feeling worried. Are we there? Are we willing to give until it hurts in order to be with our families, or do we put our own interests first? These are the questions we must ask ourselves, especially as we begin this year of the family. We must remember that love begins at home and we must also remember that "the future of humanity passes through the family."

I was surprised in the West to see so many young boys and girls given to drugs. And I tried to find out why. Why is it like that, when those in the West have so many more things than those in the East? And the answer was: "Because there is no one in the family to receive them." Our children depend on us for everything—their health, their nutrition, their security, their coming to know and love God. For all of this, they look to us with trust, hope and expectation. But often father and mother are so busy they have no time for their children, or perhaps they are not even married or have given up on their marriage. So the children go to the streets and get involved in drugs or other things. We are talking of love of the child, which is where love and peace must begin. These are the things that break peace. But I feel that the greatest destroyer of peace today is abortion, because it is a war against the child, a direct killing of the innocent child, murder by the mother herself. And if we accept that a mother can kill even her own child, how can we tell other people not to kill one another? How do we persuade a woman not to have an abortion? As always, we must persuade her with love and we remind ourselves that love means to be willing to give until it hurts. Jesus gave even His life to love us. So, the mother who is thinking of abortion, should be helped to love, that is, to give until it hurts her plans, or her free time, to respect the life of her child. The father of that child, whoever he is, must also give until it hurts.

By abortion, the mother does not learn to love, but kills even her own child to solve her problems. And, by abortion, the father is told that he does not have to take any responsibility at all for the child he has brought into the world. That father is likely to put other women into the same trouble. So abortion just leads to more abortion. Any country that accepts abortion is not teaching its people to love, but to use any violence to get what they want. This is why the greatest destroyer of love and peace is abortion.

Many people are very, very concerned with the children of India, with the children of Africa where quite a few die of hunger, and so on. Many people are also concerned about all the violence in this great country of the United States. These concerns are very good. But often these same people are not concerned with the millions who are being killed by the deliberate decision of their own mothers. And this is what is the greatest destroyer of peace today—abortion which brings people to such blindness.

And for this I appeal in India and I appeal everywhere—"Let us bring the child back." The child is God's gift to the family. Each child is created in the special image and likeness of God for greater things—to love and to be loved. In this year of the family we must bring the child back to the center of our care and concern. This is the only way that our world can survive because our children are the only hope for the future. As older people are called to God, only their children can take their places.

But what does God say to us? He says: "Even if a mother could forget her child, I will not forget you. I have carved you in the palm of my hand." We are carved in the palm of His hand; that unborn child has been carved in the hand of God from conception and is called by God to love and to be loved, not only now in this life, but forever. God can never forget us.

I will tell you something beautiful. We are fighting abortion by adoption—by care of the mother and adoption for her baby. We have saved thousands of lives. We have sent word to the clinics, to the hospitals and police stations: "Please don't destroy the child; we will take the child." So we always have someone tell the mothers in trouble: "Come, we will take care of you, we will get a home for your child." And we have a tremendous demand from couples who cannot have a child—but I never give a child to a couple who have done something not to have a child. Jesus said, "Anyone who receives a child in my name, receives me." By adopting a child, these couples receive Jesus but, by aborting a child, a couple refuses to receive Jesus.

Please don't kill the child. I want the child. Please give me the child. I am willing to accept any child who would be aborted and to give that child to a married couple who will love the child and be loved by the child. From our children's home in Calcutta alone, we have saved more than 3,000 children from abortion. These children have brought such love and joy to their adopting parents and have grown up so full of love and joy.

I know that couples have to plan their family and for that there is natural family planning. The way to plan the family is natural family planning, not contraception. In destroying the power of giving life, through contraception, a husband or wife is doing something to self. This turns the attention to self and so it destroys the gift of love in him or her. In loving, the husband and wife must turn their attention to each other as happens in natural family planning, and not to self, as happens in contraception. Once that living love is destroyed by contraception, abortion follows very easily.

I also know that there are great problems in the world—that many spouses do not love each other enough to practice natural family planning. We cannot solve all the problems in the world, but let us never bring in the worst problem of all, and that is to destroy love. And this is what happens when we tell people to practice contraception and abortion.

The poor are very great people. They can teach us so many beautiful things. Once one of them came to thank us for teaching her natural family planning and said: "You people who have practiced chastity, you are the best people to teach us natural family planning because it is nothing more than self-control out of love for each other." And what this poor person said is very true. These poor people maybe have nothing to eat, maybe they have not a home to live in, but they can still be great people when they are spiritually rich.

When I pick up a person from the street, hungry, I give him a plate of rice, a piece of bread. But a person who is shut out, who feels unwanted, unloved, terrified, the person who has been thrown out of society—that spiritual poverty is much harder to overcome. And abortion, which often follows from contraception, brings a people to be spiritually poor, and that is the worst poverty and the most difficult to overcome.

Those who are materially poor can be very wonderful people. One evening we went out and we picked up four people from the street. And one of them was in a most terrible condition. I told the Sisters: "You take care of the other three; I will take care of the one who looks worse." So I did for her all that my love can do. I put her in bed, and there was such a beautiful smile on her face. She took hold of my hand, as she said one word only: "Thank you"—and she died.

I could not help but examine my conscience before her. And I asked: "What would I say if I were in her place?" And my answer was very simple. I would have tried to draw a little attention to myself. I would have said: "I am hungry, I am dying, I am cold, I am in pain," or something. But she gave me much more—she gave me her grateful love. And she died with a smile on her face. Then there was the man we picked up from the drain, half eaten by worms and, after we had brought him to the home, he only said, "I have lived like an animal in the street, but I am going to die as an angel, loved and cared for." Then, after we had removed all the worms from his body, all he said, with a big smile, was: "Sister, I am going home to God"—and he died. It was so wonderful to see the greatness of that man who could speak like that without blaming anybody, without comparing anything. Like an angel—this is the greatness of people who are spiritually rich even when they are materially poor.

We are not social workers. We may be doing social work in the eyes of some people, but we must be contemplatives in the heart of the world. For we must bring that presence of God into your family, for the family that prays together, stays together. There is so much hatred, so much misery, and we with our prayer, with our sacrifice, are beginning at home. Love begins at home, and it is not how much we do, but how much love we put into what we do.

If we are contemplatives in the heart of the world with all its problems, these problems can never discourage us. We must always remember what God tells us in Scripture: "Even if a mother could forget the child in her womb—something impossible, but even if she could forget—I will never forget you."

And so here I am talking with you. I want you to find the poor here, right in your own home first. And begin love there. Begin that good news to your own people first. And find out about your next-door neighbors. Do you know who they are?

I had the most extraordinary experience of love of neighbor with a Hindu family. A gentleman came to our house and said: "Mother Teresa, there is a family who have not eaten for so long. Do something." So I took some rice and went there immediately. And I saw the children—their eyes shining with hunger. I don't know if you have ever seen hunger. But I have seen it very often. And the mother of the family took the rice I gave her and went out. When she came back, I asked her: "Where did you go? What did you do?" and she gave me a very simple answer: "They are hungry also." What struck me was that she knew—

and who are they? A Muslim family—and she knew. I didn't bring any more rice that evening because I wanted them, Hindus and Muslims, to enjoy the joy of sharing.

But there were those children, radiating joy, sharing the joy and peace with their mother because she had the love to give until it hurts. And you see this is where love begins—at home in the family.

So, as the example of this family shows, God will never forget us and there is something you and I can always do. We can keep the joy of loving Jesus in our hearts, and share that joy with all we come in contact with. Let us make that one point—that no child will be unwanted, unloved, uncared for, or killed and thrown away. And give until it hurts—with a smile.

Because I talk so much of giving with a smile, once a professor from the United States asked me: "Are you married?" And I said: "Yes, and I find it sometimes very difficult to smile at my Spouse, Jesus, because He can be very demanding—sometimes." This is really something true. And there is where love comes in—when it is demanding, and yet we can give it with joy.

One of the most demanding things for me is travelling everywhere—and with publicity. I have said to Jesus that if I don't go to heaven for anything else, I will be going to heaven for all the travelling with all the publicity, because it has purified me and sacrificed me and made me really ready to go to heaven.

If we remember that God loves us, and that we can love others as He loves us, then America can become a sign of peace for the world. From here, a sign of care for the weakest of the weak—the unborn child—must go out to the world. If you become a burning light of justice and peace in the world, then really you will be true to what the founders of this country stood for. God bless you!

1. Describe what Mother Teresa says about children.
2. Why does the unborn child matter, according to Mother Teresa?
3. How would Mother Teresa depict a good marriage?

Index

About the Editor

Matthew Levering is associate professor of theology at Ave Maria University in Naples, Florida. His other volumes in this series include *On the Priesthood, On Christian Dying,* and *On Prayer and Contemplation.* He is author of *Scripture and Metaphysics* and *Christ's Fulfillment of Torah and Temple,* and is coauthor of *Knowing the Love of Christ* and *Holy People, Holy Land.* He has most recently edited *Reading John with St. Thomas Aquinas.* He serves as coeditor of the theological quarterly *Nova et Vetera.*